75¢

Discovering
TENNESSEE
STATE PARKS

Discovering

TENNESSEE

STATE PARKS

A Guide to the State Parks in Tennessee

J.L. & Lin Stepp

MOUNTAIN HILL PRESS

Mountain Hill Press

A Division of S & S Communications

Discovering Tennessee State Parks
Copyright @2018
James L. Stepp

Cover Design by Katherine E. Stepp
Cover Photos by J.L. and Lin Stepp
Book Design and Layout by Mountain Hill Press
Editorial Assistance by Elizabeth S. James
Interior Photos by J.L and Lin Stepp

Published by Mountain Hill Press
A division of S & S Communications

Author note. This is a non-fiction guidebook created by the authors based on their visitations and research of Tennessee State Parks. Effort has been made to ensure accuracy of specific environs and place names, but places and names may change over time as do descriptive trail details.

Library of Congress Cataloging-in-Publication Data

Stepp, J.L. and Lin
    Discovering Tennessee State Parks: A Guide to the State Parks in Tennessee
    by J.L. and Lin Stepp
    ISBN 978-0-9985063-2-6
    eISBN 978-0-9985063-5-7

Non-Fiction. 1. State Parks—Tennessee—Guidebooks. 2. Parks—Southeast—Guide
    books. 3. Travel—Tennessee—Guidebooks.
    I. Stepp, J.L. and Lin II. Title
    Library of Congress Control Number: 2018933100

ACKNOWLEDGMENTS

Thanks and gratitude goes to the Tennessee State Parks office, under the banner of Tennessee's Department of Environment and Conservation, located in Nashville, Tennessee. We are deeply grateful for:
- their mission to manage, protect, and preserve scenic areas in our state;
- their excellent state park website detailing each of the fifty-six parks, which helped us with the accuracy of our book;
- their careful and meticulous care in designing and maintaining all the parks throughout the state of Tennessee, making each a delight to visit.

Appreciation and thanks also goes to:
- the park rangers and visitor center staff members in each park we visited who answered our questions, helped us with information, and gave us tips on special places to see while visiting the parks;
- the staff in the park lodges where we stayed overnight, at restaurants in the parks where we often caught a quick lunch, and in the golf pro shops we visited. All were welcoming, gracious, and eager to provide helpful tips for our book.

For additional information about Tennessee's state parks, see the park website at: *http://tnstateparks.com/*

Great Smoky Mountains Scenes

Introduction

In October 2013, the United States (U.S.) Government shut down all 401 national parks across the country, closing every park, battlefield, monument, and historic house under its jurisdiction. For us, as avid hikers in the Great Smoky Mountains National Park near our home, that meant no hikes or outdoor adventures for a while, and no one knew how long the closures would last.

Looking for alternative outdoor options, we decided to check out the state parks in Tennessee, which were still open. The state website provided information about each park but we wanted a book to take in hand, to read and study about the different ones individually. We located a few small books, often focusing on area history, but not the type of park-by-park guidebook we hoped for. So we decided to write one.

We had enjoyed working together to hike trails in the Great Smoky Mountains National Park to create our hiking guidebook *The Afternoon Hiker*, published in 2014, and we had been looking for a new adventure. After a season of research and planning, while getting other ongoing works and publications finalized, we started our exploration of Tennessee parks in the summer of 2015. We decided to visit the parks in an east to west order, beginning in the far eastern end of Tennessee and moving across to the state's western end along the Mississippi River.

The first park we visited was Warriors' Path State Park in Kingsport on July 16, 2015. In the same month we visited three more parks—Sycamore Shoals, Davy Crockett, and Roan Mountain—and we were hooked. We also felt amazed to realize how little we knew about Tennessee's state parks, all right in our back door, and how beautiful they were. Every tract held new adventures, sights, trails, historic spots, lovely lakes, old mills, mountains, interesting wildlife, flowers, and more. Visiting each felt like taking a mini-vacation every time we set out as every park offered its own unique experiences and appeal. The more we traveled and explored, the more fun we had. Three quarters of the parks were close enough to our home to drive to and return in a day. Later we stayed at picturesque park lodges, whenever possible, as we explored the parks further west.

This book *Discovering Tennessee State Parks* records our journey and park visits. It is also a guidebook for others who want to visit and explore any or all of Tennessee's parks. With each park visited, we included directions to get to the site, a description of the park, its sections and amenities, trails to hike, things to do and see, and the month of the year we visited—since different seasons offer different pleasures. In addition, we included hundreds of color photos throughout the book of special scenes in every park to give readers a flavor of what they might see at their visits. We hope you will use and cherish this book as you tour and enjoy the incredible variety of parks scattered across the state of Tennessee.

TENNESSEE STATE PARKS

PASSPORT

Protecting Tennessee's natural and
cultural resources for over 75 years

TENNESSEE
State Parks

www.tnstateparks.com

If you plan to visit many—or all—of
Tennessee's state parks, pick up a free
Tennessee State Parks Passport book at
a visitor center. Inside you can note the
date you visited the park, memories you
want to recall from your visit ... and get
a staff member to stamp your book with
a unique seal.

TABLE OF CONTENTS

HISTORY OF STATE PARKS

The history of the state parks and national parks are intertwined. State parks, like national ones, were established to preserve locations of natural beauty and recreational potential and to safeguard places of historic significance. The first national park, Yellowstone National Park, was established by an Act of Congress in 1872 and signed by President Ulysses Grant, beginning the national parks movement. More parks followed, especially out west, before southern ones began to develop. President Theodore Roosevelt was a great champion in advancing the national park movement, and many bird and game preserves, national forests, parks, and monuments were established during his presidency. His cousin, Franklin Delano Roosevelt, would later formally dedicate the Great Smoky Mountains National Park in 1940.

The first state park was Niagara Falls State Park, established in 1885, with a few others following in the late 1800s and early 1900s. In 1921, at the request of Stephen Mather, the National Park Service Director, a group of preservationists and conservationists met in Iowa to discuss the concept of developing additional parks at the state level. This 1921 National Conference of State Parks, hosted by the National Park Service, spurred interest in developing more sites around America and initiated the state park movement. At the time of the conference 29 states, including Tennessee, had no state parks, but by 1925, all 48 states had begun to formulate development plans. Although the beginning of the Depression slowed growth, many recreational areas were developed later in the 1930s through Depression-era programs like the Civilian Conservation Corps (CCC), Works Progress Administration (WPA), and the Tennessee Valley Authority (TVA). States around the U.S. recognized that lands needed to be preserved at the local level that would not become designated as national sites. By 1972, every state in the U.S. had a state parks system.

Tennessee's state parks, like others in America, were created to preserve and protect unique recreational, historic, cultural, and scenic natural areas. The first in Tennessee, Harrison Bay State Park near Chattanooga, was opened in 1937. Other early state parks like Norris Dam, Big Ridge, and Cove Lake were created in conjunction with TVA's impoundment of lakes in order to build dams. Some park lands were donated to Tennessee by industrial companies, gained from other state agencies, or purchased. By 1962, Tennessee had 20 state parks and by 2017, there were 56. The two newest are Rocky Fork, added in 2012 and Seven Islands State Birding Park added in 2013.

In 2017, the Tennessee State Park (TSP) system celebrated its 80th anniversary. According to the TSP website Tennessee's 56 state parks contain 1,100 miles of trails, 36 campgrounds, 365 cabins, hundreds of lakes, and over 80 waterfalls. Tennessee State Parks was named a finalist for the 2017 Gold Medal Awards in Excellence in Parks and Recreation Management, a prestigious state honor. Parks in Tennessee are open year round,

although some have shortened hours during holidays and not all amenities are open year round, such as swimming pools. No admission fees are charged to visit any Tennessee park, making it one of only seven states that receive no money from park entrance fees. Discounts are also available for many features, like cabin rentals, stays at park lodges, golf or other sporting activities, and reduced fees are offered to seniors, active military, veterans, and members of associations like the American Association of Retired Persons (AARP). On an interesting note, statistics show that state parks in the United States (U.S.) serve two and a half times as many visitors as the national parks with only 16 percent of the acreage.

Throughout the U.S., and in Tennessee, state parks are a treasure often unappreciated or applauded. They give Americans a place to get out-of-doors for recreation and pleasure in locales close to their homes. The scenic areas benefit individuals by creating opportunities for family bonding, relieving stress, and providing peaceful time in nature. Parks provide economic and ecological value and conserve environmental and historic riches that might otherwise have been lost. They serve as a catalyst for tourism, provide activities for youth leisure, offer recreational venues for groups, and are a rich source of pride for individual states and their communities. Franklin D. Roosevelt wrote *"The nation that destroys its soil, destroys itself"* and many other leaders have realized the value of conserving lands and waters for future generations. Tennessee's state parks offer opportunity for all its citizens to enjoy time out of doors in beautiful locations.

"Keep close to Nature's heart...and break clear away, once in a while, and climb a mountain or spend a week in the woods. Wash your spirit clean." – John Muir

Roan Mountain

EAST TENNESSEE STATE PARK INDEX

EAST
TENNESSEE
PARKS

Big Ridge

Hiwassee/Ocoee Rivers

Frozen Head

Harrison Bay

Warriors' Path State Park

East Tennessee - Sullivan County
Park Address: 490 Hemlock Road, Kingsport, TN 37663
Park Size: 950 Acres   Month Visited: July
Directions: From I-81 take exit 59; turn on Ft Henry Drive/State
Route 36; Turn Right on Hemlock Drive (park sign on left after
turn); Continue straight; after driving under an overpass, watch for
park entrance on left.

Park Description:

This beautiful state park is located on the TVA Patrick Henry Reservoir in northeast Tennessee on a bend of the South Fork Holston River. Ready access to—and enjoyment of—the waterfront is a hallmark of this scenic park. A fine marina offers boat rentals, fishing piers, launch ramps for pleasure boating, skiing, or fishing, and a shady family picnic area nestles on a hillside nearby.

On Duck Island, directly across from the marina, is a fine modern recreation center with indoor facilities, tennis courts, a basketball court, outdoor shelters for group and family events, and a second picnic area. A paved pathway, seven tenths of a mile long, circles around Duck Island providing an accessible lakeside trail for biking or walking.

On first entering Warriors' Path, be sure to stop at the small gray headquarters office to pick up brochures and to get a map of the grounds. For pre-planning, information and maps can also be found on the Tennessee State Parks website. A short distance above the headquarters office on the hill is a large, Olympic-sized swimming pool. The fenced pool has changing rooms, outdoor chairs and tables, a fun water slide, and a lifeguard on duty. Not far from the pool is a tiered outdoor amphitheater where many activities and events are held. Rangers and staff members take visitors on guided hikes, give nature talks, and offer hands-on arts and craft activities.

The main campground with over a hundred RV and tent campsites lies along a loop road on the peninsula in the river's bend. The campsites are shady and well maintained, all with tables and grills, and most are equipped with water and electrical hookups. Within the camp area are restrooms, a bathhouse, and dump stations. The campground is very popular with visitors and reservations should be made in advance of arrival. These can be made by phone or

email up to twelve months ahead, with discounts for seniors, veterans, and state employees.

An unusual and charming spot at Warriors' Path State Park is the Darrell's Dream Boundless Playground for children, opened in 2007. Located just past the marina, the playground provides a wonderland of shady walkways and play structures along the banks of a small creek. Within the area is the giant Anderson Tree House, a delight for children to play in, and winding around the playground on a quarter mile trail are interactive points telling the story of Aslan

the Lion in *The Chronicles of Narnia*. Statuaries sit along the trail side, like the White Stag and Mr. Tumnus, helping to bring the story to life. For adults, there are scenic benches and a covered picnic pavilion to enjoy while watching the children play. This is one of the loveliest playgrounds we've ever seen within a state park—well worth a visit by itself.

Warriors' Park has ten maintained hiking trails. Four are short hikes within the interior of the park, easy walks around the campground and along the water's edge. These are the half mile Lakeshore Trail, the 0.75 mile Lake Hollow Trail, the 0.75 mile Connector Trail, and the half mile Riverbank Trail. Combining three of these trails,

15

Warriors' Path State Park:

- RV or tent Campsites * Picnic Area * Camp Store and Snack Bars
* Marina * Boat Rentals, Paddleboats and Canoes * Boat Launch Ramps
* Fishing Piers * 18 Hole Golf Course * Riding Stable
* Tennis Courts, Archery, Disc Golf, Soccer fields * Children's Playground
* Swimming Pool * Hiking Trails and Nature Walks * Mtn Bike Trails

the Lakeshore, Connector and Lake Hollow trails, provides a two-miles loop around the campground. A fifth hike, the Holston Bluff Loop Trail, begins behind the Overflow Campground to wind along a ridge overlooking the pretty Ft. Patrick Henry Reservoir. Another walk to enjoy, the Devil's Backbone Trail, begins on the left of Fall Creek Road after crossing the bridge over the Holston River. A pull-over parking area is on the right of the road and the sign at the trail's beginning is clearly visible. This trail (2.5 mi) is a more strenuous one, climbing to some fine ridge overlooks before dipping down to Fall Creek and an area where early settlers once lived. To add to this walk, hikers can continue on around the 1.5 miles Fall Creek Loop Trail, creating a 6.5 miles roundtrip hike. A trails map, available at the park headquarters office, describes the hikes and has a diagram to help locate them. We hiked sections of the Lakeshore Loop in the campground area and up the Devil's Backbone Trail on our visit. These trails were all easy to locate, had clear park signs, and were well maintained.

For those preferring biking to hiking, the park has an internationally renowned mountain bike trail system on 150 acres, designed and built by mountain bikers. Using directions picked up in the headquarters office, follow approximately five miles to the backside of the river to find the parking area at the end of Freeman Road for the nine miles of biking trails. There are Beginner, Intermediate, and Advanced routes for every biker level and the bike trail system is a designated National Recreation Trail area.

Two additional pluses available at Warriors' State Park are a riding stables and a fine 18-hole par

72 golf course designed by George Cobb. This course is one of the most popular in the Tennessee State Parks system with wide fairways and a lot of hazards, a driving range, pro shop, and ample parking.

Fishing is good on the reservoir year-round with largemouth and smallmouth bass the primary game, along with crappie, catfish, and trout. Visitors can enjoy fishing out on the lake, along the banks, and at the nice fishing piers. Fishing derbys and events are often held at Warriors' Path, along with other popular annual events including a Winter Garden Seminar, a Spring Nature Festival, and a Summer Folklife Festival. For a week-long or weekend stay, or for a single day visit, this state park tucked around the banks of the scenic Holston River offers many entertaining amenities.

History Note:
In America's early days, a native American trading and warpath, called the Great Cherokee War and Trading Path, wound near the area where the park now lies— inspiring the park's unusual name. As settlers traveled into the Tennessee area, they followed the Indian pathways. Many of these old trails developed into roads, and later interstate routes, while others formed hiking trails and quiet roadways in state and national parks. A historical marker can be found in front of the Recreation Center citing that the early trading path was one of the most heavily traveled roads in Colonial America.

Sycamore Shoals State Historic Park

East Tennessee - Carter Conty
Park Address: 1651 West Elk Avenue, Elizabethton, TN 37643
Park Size: 70 Acres   Month Visited: July
Directions: From exit 57 on I-81, take I-26 into Johnson City to Exit 24. Then take Hwy 321/67 for approximately 6 miles, which becomes Elk Avenue. Sycamore Shoals is on the left just before the hospital.

Park Description:

Sycamore Shoals, like many parks in the Tennessee State Park system, was established primarily as a state historic area since several significant historical events occurred here. In 1772, the first permanent settlement outside the thirteen English colonies was established at Sycamore Shoals and in 1780 the Overmountain Men mustered here before marching to King's Mountain to defeat British forces.

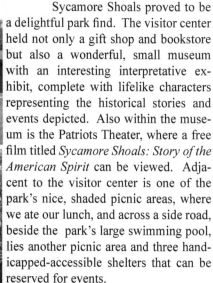

Sycamore Shoals proved to be a delightful park find. The visitor center held not only a gift shop and bookstore but also a wonderful, small museum with an interesting interpretative exhibit, complete with lifelike characters representing the historical stories and events depicted. Also within the museum is the Patriots Theater, where a free film titled *Sycamore Shoals: Story of the American Spirit* can be viewed. Adjacent to the visitor center is one of the park's nice, shaded picnic areas, where we ate our lunch, and across a side road, beside the park's large swimming pool, lies another picnic area and three handicapped-accessible shelters that can be reserved for events.

A winding two miles round trip hiking trail, called the Mountain River Trail, winds along the south bank of the Watauga River at the back of the park. The gravel trail provides a delightful, easy walk through the woods along the banks of the river. Along the pathway are interpretive signs telling about historical events related to the park. Fly fishing, angling, canoeing and kayaking are available on the river, as well, but the park does not have campground facilities for overnight stays.

The highlight of the Sycamore Shoals State Park is the large realistic replica of Fort Watauga in the center of the park grounds. The fort has several furnished structures and cabins inside it that offer a true sense of what 18th century life on the frontier was like. Beside the fort is a historic muster grounds with park benches around it, and behind the fort is Sycamore Shoals' 240-seat outdoor amphitheater.

Many outdoor events are held here, including the annual outdoor drama *Liberty! A Saga of Sycamore Shoals*. This official drama, presented by local performers in full period costume, tells the story of the early colonists who settled the area. They fought to establish their homes in the wilderness, made treaties with the Cherokee Indians, and sacrificed to help gain America's independence. Other events held during the year at Sycamore Shoals include nature events, an annual Celtic Festival, a commemorative celebration in September to honor the contributions of the Overmountain Men, quilt and art shows, old time craft days, a Colonial Harvest Celebration in November, and a variety of other historical and natural programs throughout the year.

History Note:

In 1780, the Patriot militia learned that the British Loyalists under Major Patrick Ferguson were retreating through North Carolina. Nine hundred select Patriots mustered at Sycamore Shoals before setting out in pursuit of Ferguson's Loyalists. The Patriots caught the Loyalists by surprise and defeated them at the Battle of Kings Mountain on October 7, 1780. This was a decisive victory in the American Revolutionary War and a turning point in the war's effort. Thomas Jefferson called it "the turn of the tide of success."

19

David Crockett Birthplace State Park

East Tennessee - Greene County
Park Address: 1245 Davy Crockett Park Road, Limestone, TN 37681
Park Size: 105 Acres   Month Visited: July
Directions: From I-81, follow signs at exit 23 through Greeneville to park, approximately 27 miles.

Park Description:

The David Crockett State Park was created as a memorial to David (Davy) Crockett, a famous frontiersman, soldier and politician. Crockett was born in 1786 in a log cabin on the Nolichucky River in Limestone, in what is

now known as Greene County, and grew up in East Tennessee. After a long career as a farmer, scout, soldier, public official, businessman, member of the Tennessee General Assembly and the U.S. House of Representatives, Crockett fought at the Battle of the Alamo, where he died in 1836.

The most prominent part of the park is a replica of the cabin Davy Crockett was born in, created on a site not far from the banks of the Nolichucky River. It is a simple one-room structure with few windows, one chimney and a small porch. A footstone, supposedly from the original Crockett cabin that was torn down, sits behind the building as does a picnic pavilion looking toward the river. On the farm site in front of the cabin is a rough garden plot, an outdoor cooking and demonstration area, and a stone monument. A tall, historic limestone marker sits in the midst of a circular wall of limestone blocks, which contains native stones from all 50 states in the U.S. Several signs and markers around the farm site tell facts and show pictures of Crockett's life and career as a pioneer, hunter, and statesman.

On the hillside above the farm site is a visitor center and park office. The visitor center contains a small gift shop and a museum with artifacts and

displays about Crockett's life. A film about his life can also be viewed. During the summer, rangers offer historical and cultural programs for visitors. In August the park hosts Crockett Days with history demonstrations, period costumes, music, food, crafts, games and other activities. In other seasons of

the year the park offers a variety of pioneer arts events and workshops, and in October a bluegrass and barbeque festival is held on the grounds.

For a quiet place in which to camp and get away from it all, David Crockett Park is a good choice. There is a shady campground on the river with eighty-eight campsites, most with full hookups for water, electric, and sewer. A large swimming pool, covered pavilion, and children's playground lie just across the road from the campground. There are also three picnic pavilions on the grounds, a basketball court, and several short hiking trails. We hiked

the trail along the Nolichucky River on our visit and walked along the riverbank where we found many scenic picnic spots and saw visitors wading and playing in the water. The park has a boat ramp, and fishing is good on the Nolichucky River whiich flows through the park. The rural location provides good biking within the grounds and along country roads in the surrounding area.

History Note.

During his lifetime Davy Crockett's reputation as a frontiersman, hunter, and tale-spinner helped to elevate him to folk legend status. Stories and books were written about him and he became known as the "King of the Wild Frontier," easily recognized by his famous buckskin clothing and coonskin cap. Several songs were composed about Crockett, including "The Ballad of Davy Crockett," and two movies and a weekly television-series were created by Walt Disney about his life, starring Fess Parker as Davy.

Roan Mountain State Park

East Tennessee - Carter County
Park Address: 1015 Hwy 143, Roan Mountain, TN 37687
Park Size: 2,006 Acres   Month Visited: July
Directions: From I-81 take I-26 Johnson City Exit to Elizabethton
Exit, Hwy 321. From Elizabethton take Hwy 19E approximately
16 miles to Hwy 143. Turn right on Hwy 143 leading directly into
the Roan Mountain State Park. From Elk Park, NC, take Hwy
19E to Roan Mountain and turn on Hwy 143.

Park Description:

This beautiful park lies in a high elevation area at the base of Roan Mountain, feeling more like the Smoky Mountains than other parks we visited. The Doe River winds through the park, more of a gurgling mountain stream than a river in appearance. An attractive visitor center lies on the left just past the entrance. A walkway crosses the Doe River to the main visitor center with a rustic, old mill wheel beside the bridge. There are rocking chairs and a picnic table on the visitor center's broad porch, and we ate our lunch there beside the river. Inside the center are a gift shop and a small museum. Outside is a second museum room related to the Peg Leg Iron Ore Mine, which operated near this site in the 1800s. We walked the Peg Leg Mine Trail back through the woods to the remains of the old

mine entrance—a nice hike less than a mile round trip in length.

Within the Roan Mountain State Park are all the amenities most tourists could hope for. The park has a lovely, shady campground area along the Doe River with 107 sites, 87 for RVs, bathhouses, and a cute camp store. For entertainment, there are playgrounds, a huge pool, volleyball, horseshoes, ping-pong, basketball, softball, tennis, a game room and several picnic pavilions. There is also a large modern conference center, an amphitheater, and thirty rental cabins.

The cabins are well-equipped and nicely furnished with grills, and all have big front porches with rocking chairs. Throughout the park are 12 miles of hiking trails and two mountain bike trails.

After winding past the visitor center into the park, watch for the road on the right that travels a mile up Strawberry Mountain to the Miller Farmstead. The Miller family farmed the land on this high mountain site for three generations. The park has preserved the historic property and a staff member is usually on site to tell you the farm's history. The farmstead, nestled in an idyllic setting, contains the old white Miller farmhouse, a large barn, a springhouse, smokehouse and other outbuildings, with fruit trees and a garden plot. Just up the road from the farm and

down a short gravel road is the family cemetery and the beginning of the Chestnut Ridge Trail. At the start of the trail is a wooden overlook platform with fabulous views out over Roan Mountain. We enjoyed the views and then hiked a length of the trail out across the ridge top in an area heavy with grapevines draped across the trees.

Returning from the farmstead to the main road and then continuing on leads to the busier area of the state park—to the campground, cabins, picnic pavilions, amphitheater, conference center, pool, and play areas. The Doe River wanders merrily throughout all with walking bridges across it at many points. Fishing is popular on the river and rainbow, brook and brown trout are stocked regularly. We hiked the Riverside Trail that travels along behind the campground

Roan Mountain State Park:

• Conference Center * Cabins * Swimming Pool * Picnic Pavilions
* Playgrounds * Fishing * Camping - RV Sites * Hiking/Biking Trails
* Interpretive/Visitor's Center * Gift Shop * Museum
* Planned Programs * Amphitheater

area along the Doe River and we also hiked the Tom Gray Trail, just beyond the camp store nearer the end of the park. This was an especially pleasant trail with scenic rest benches built in several spots alongside the river.

Like most large, developed state parks, Roan Mountain hosts a variety of programs and activities year round. These include organized hikes, nature studies, games, entertainment, fishing tournaments, and musical events at the amphitheater and the Miller Farmstead, to name only a few. Several annual festivals are also held, the most famous of which is the Rhododendron Festival in the third weekend in June. This festival celebrates the blooming season of the Catawba rhododendron on Roan Mountain, about 9-10 miles south of the park at the top of the mountain. Leaving the park, the highway continues up to Carver's Gap on the crest of the mountain to a well-marked sign to the gardens. A road to the right leads out to a parking area for the Rhododendron Gardens. This is the largest natural rhododendron garden in the world with sweeps of rhododendron in bloom in peak season. An accessible walkway leads through the gardens and down the Cloudland Trail to an observation platform looking out over the valley below. The Roan Mountain ranges are some of the highest ranges in the Southeast, with peaks over 6,000 feet, and the views from the top of the mountain are breathtaking.

On the other side of Carver's Gap is a parking area with a trail leading out to the Grassy Ridge. There are seven miles of grassy bald, or high meadows with sparse trees, that spread over three mountain summits here. The Appalachian Trail also crosses the Roan Mountain crest and visitors can walk sections of it while visiting at the state park. Many hikers claim this is the most beautiful part of the Appalachian Trail with alpine like meadows, glorious flowers, and stunning views.

History Note.
General John Wilder (1830-1917), an officer in the Union Army and an industrialist, was the first to develop the Roan Mountain area. Wilder founded ironworks in several areas of Tennessee and then in 1870 bought 7,000 acres around Roan Mountain for approximately $25 an acre and started mining iron ore in the area. One of his mines became known as the Peg Leg Mine, the remains of which you can still see in the park. The Miller Farmstead and other farmland was once owned by Wilder, but he later sold much of it. On his property at the top of Roan

Mountain, Wilder built a luxury three-storied resort called the Cloudland Hotel. It was a glorious place in its time with a grand ballroom and elegant furnishings and many famous people and dignitaries stayed there to enjoy the cool mountain air and wonderful meals before the hotel declined and was later destroyed in the 1900s. We marveled that the entire Roan Mountain area had once belonged to only one man.

Panther Creek State Park

East Tennessee - Hamblen County
Park Address: 2010 Panther Creek Park Road. Morristown, TN 37814
Park Size: 1,435 Acres   Month Visited: August
Directions: From Hwy 11E, between Jefferson City and Morristown, turn onto Hwy 342 at Park Sign and travel approximately 2.5 miles to entrance of park on the right at Panther Creek Road.

Park Description:

The Panther Creek State Park sprawls on a lush 1,435 acres property along the shores of Cherokee Lake. We expected the property to have lakeside picnic tables, waterfront camping, and extensive access to the lake but the park property lies instead high on ridges above the lake, providing many stunning views over the Cherokee Reservoir. The park is a lovely wilderness preserve with opportunities for fishing, birding, and simply enjoying the beauty of the natural area, including forests, trails, spectacular views, wildflowers, and wildlife.

A visitor center sits on the left inside the main entrance, where park information, maps, and trail guides can be attained. Beyond the visitor center is a fine Olympic-sized pool on the hillside, tennis courts, and a beautiful children's park with great swings and play structures. Across the road from the recreation area is a big soccer field and behind the field, a small bridge leading across to a nature loop trail, nice for any age to enjoy. This 1.2 miles trail was awarded the Governor's Greenways and Trails Stewardship Award in 2004.

The park campground lies just off the main road on a loop winding through a quiet wooded area. There are 50 tent or trailer campsites with water and electrical hookups. Each has a picnic table and grill and there is a laundry, two bathhouses, and a dump station. Beyond the campground is the Spoone Shelter area with a covered pavilion and 14 public picnic tables. All the tables sit around a shaded hillside with interesting rock formations scattered behind them. We ate our lunch here and then hiked two of the trails that begin out of the area.

For those who love to hike, Panther Creek has more than 30 miles of hiking trails, 16 different trails listed on the park's trail guide. Several of the trails are also biking and horse trails. From out of the Spoone Shelter area we hiked the Ore Mine Trail, a 1.3 miles loop that leads through an area where manganese mining was done in the 1800s. Manganese was used to make steel and glass, and we found a few rocks along the path with bits of the shiny ore in them. Even more interesting to explore was the Seven Sinkholes Loop Trail. This 0.6 mile trail climbs up a ridge and passes beside seven natural sinkholes—each unique and so fascinating to see. Some were large enough to walk down into. This was our favorite trail in the park.

Panther Creek State Park:

* Visitor Center   * Picnic Area   * Fishing   *   Boat Launch Ramp
* Bike Trails   * Tennis Courts   * Playgrounds   * Hiking Trails
* Swimming Pool   * RV Campsites

A little further beyond Spoone Shelter is one of two parking areas for horse trailers, providing access to trails designated for horseback riding, the Maple Arch Trail and the Hunt Knob Trail, which hikers can also enjoy for longer hikes. We walked across the road from the park area, crossing Panther

Creek on a wooden bridge, to hike up the Old Wagon Trail into the woods on a flat, wide road-bed. This is an easy one-mile trail suitable for biking and for family walks. Another trail that begins out of the parking area is The Point Lookout Trail Loop. This 1.9 miles hike ascends to the highest elevation in the park at 1,460 feet above sea level to arrive at a rocky overlook above the Cherokee Lake. We hiked to the overlook but found the views obscured by trees in August, somewhat disappointing after the long, difficult trek to the top.

A more accessible—and much better—panoramic view of the lake can be found further up the road at the Smallman picnic area and pavilion. This scenic area sits high on a hillside overlooking the Cherokee Lake. A wooden observatory has been built right beside the road where you can enjoy stunning views out across the lake, of several islands, and to the shore and land beyond. This would be a great spot to plan a picnic or group gathering. At the end of the loop road lies another trail, the Ridge Crest Trail, which journeys 0.7 mile down-

hill to the lakeside. It's steep and the hike back up proves even more strenuous than the walk down.

Before leaving the park, we drove down to the park's boat launch ramp. Although not very large, and without facilities like a marina, this spot provides a nice place for launching boats, canoes, or other watercraft with ample parking available. A short distance beyond the side road to the boat ramp, is a second parking area for horse trailers and bike trail parking. We saw two horseback riders on one of the nice trails in this area and we spotted the trailheads for several other hiking trails along the road to the ramp. We checked out all of them and then hiked a portion of the two mile Trout Lily Trail, famous for trout lily wildflowers along the pathways from March to May.

Like most state parks, Panther Creek hosts seasonal activities for visitors, like guided walks to the Creek Observation Deck or to the Norris Blackburn Wildlife Observatory. Canoe trips are offered as well as evening campfires and nature activities. Being avid hikers, we were especially delighted by the great diversity of hiking and walking trails throughout the entire park, and we explored eight while visiting.

History Note.

Panther Creek was one of the earliest settlements in Hamblen County. Many settlers lived in the area with a store, post office, blacksmith, tavern, school, church and a popular spring—all on a well-traveled stagecoach route. The name Panther Creek came from an old story about an early settler who killed a panther which fell in the creek. We were interested to learn that the Panther Creek community was once larger and more populated than Morristown but lost its prominence after the railroads came.

Big Ridge State Park

East Tennessee - Union County
Park Address: 1015 Big Ridge Park Rd, Maynardville, TN 37807
Park Size: 3,687 Acres   Month Visited: August
Directions: From I-75 Exit 122 take Hwy 61 east for approximately 12 miles to the park entrance on the left between Andersonville and Maynardville.

Park Description:

Big Ridge State Park lies about 35 miles north of Knoxville on Norris Lake. The park was built in the 1930s after the construction of Norris Dam and reservoir to illustrate the recreational opportunities possible on the new lakeshores. The Tennessee Valley Authority (TVA) operated the park until 1949 when Big Ridge was transferred to the parks system.

The main developed portion of Big Ridge lies on a peninsula tucked between two fingers of Norris Lake—although the full acreage of the park sprawls beyond this area to the north, east, and south. We found it a pleasure to revisit this familiar state park nearer our home and enjoyed discovering aspects of it that we'd never explored before.

At the visitor center, guests can pick up a park map, a hiking trail guide and see a topographical replica of the area grounds under glass. Near the visitor center is a recreational area with a large children's playground, volleyball, basketball, tennis courts, and a softball field. The road to the campground is nearby, winding south to 50 campsites for tent, trailer and RV camping with restrooms, bathhouses, and a dump station. Across the lake from the end of the campground the boat ramp can be seen. Family biking is popular on the shady roads through the campground and throughout the park.

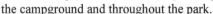

On the hillside near the visitor center are picnic tables and two pavilions that look down over the lake. A highlight of Big Ridge State Park is the beautiful sandy beach and swim area created on one of the fingers of the lake. There is a bathhouse on a rise, leading out to a rolling green lawn overlooking the swimming beach and Big Ridge Lake. The swim area's large shallow end has rock steps for entry and a concrete bottom, and the intermediate and deeper lake areas have big rafts for swimmers to enjoy.

A short walk or drive from the beach area leads to a fine recreation hall on a hillside looking across the lake where weddings, reunions, and other events are often held. It is a beautiful old structure and has a deep covered porch and

long windows to catch the views. Below the recreation hall is the boat dock where paddleboats, canoes, or rowboats can be rented. With so much lake access, fishing is great along the banks on the Big Ridge Lake or from personal watercraft on Norris Lake. The area is famous for striped bass, black bass, and bream, and the Waterside and Hickory Star marinas for fishing boat or pontoon rentals on Norris Lake are not far away.

Near the Big Ridge Park boat dock, a wooden bridge leads to a second shaded picnic area with nice tables and a third covered picnic shelter. The park's

Big Ridge State Park:
* Visitor Center * Picnic Area * Fishing * Boat Launch Ramp
* Water Skiing * Tennis Courts * Playgrounds * Hiking Trails
* Swimming * RV Campsites * Back Country Camping * Gift Shop

cabins lie tucked off the roads nearby. The park has 19 cabins scattered along winding back roads in the woods and along the lakeside for weekly rental. Built in the 1930s, the one-bedroom cabins have a special rustic charm with rich wood paneling and old rock fireplaces inside. Each cabin has a big screened porch looking out into the woods or across the lake.

Many families once lived on the park's land before Norris Dam was built, and remnants of those families and their community can still be found. The Norton Gristmill, originally constructed in the 1800s, still stands on the grounds. One of the area hiking trails, the Old Mill Trail, branches out behind it. The park has 11 hiking trails, scattered around the property, all well-maintained. We hiked the Old Mill Trail curling along the lakeside, the Chestnut Ridge Trail near the cabin area, part of the Big Valley Trail, and we climbed to Meditation Point at the end of the day. The park also has three backcountry campsites and a group camp area—not far from the Norton Mill—with 18 screened-in bunkhouses ideal for youth events.

Our favorite trail at Big Ridge State Park was the Lake Trail, which

winds around the perimeter of Big Ridge Lake, crossing over the old wooden dam that protects the 50 acre lake. We hiked the eastern end of the Lake Trail from the group camp area to the dam and back, approximately two miles roundtrip. The trail crosses several manmade bridges as it winds its way through a peaceful woods, then follows along the lake for much of the latter part of its journey to the old dam. Approximately midway to the Big Ridge Dam, a side hike climbs up to the old Snodderly Cemetery where we found the gravesites of early settlers of the 1800s, such as Snodderlys, McCoys, and Troxlers. Several other trails in the park also lead to old cemeteries and early settlement areas, to the remnants of Sharp's Station Fort, and to scenic overlooks across the lake.

The park hosts a popular Bluegrass Festival in August every year, an Easter Egg Hunt in spring, and Ghost Walks in October on the Ghost House Trail leading to the old home site and grave of Maston Hutchison. This lovely state park is readily accessible with pleasurable aspects for all ages. On the August weekday we visited, we luckily had much of the park to ourselves.

History Note:

At Big Ridge's entry is a small stone house that once served as the park office. It is a fine example of the craftsmanship of the Civilian Conservation Corps (CCC) who helped to construct the park. Throughout the park are old walls, bridges, and other buildings that show the handiwork of the Corps. A plaque at the old park office gives tribute to the work of the CCC, a program established in 1933 by President Franklin Roosevelt that provided employment for millions and which improved the country's natural resources at the same time. The CCC and the Tennessee Valley Authority (TVA) combined with the National Park Service to create and build Big Ridge State Park.

Fort Loudoun State Historic Park

East Tennessee - Monroe County
Park Address: 338 Fort Loudoun Road, Vonore, TN 37885
Park Size: 1,200 Acres   Month Visited: August
Directions: From I40/75 take I-140 to Hwy 129 south to Hwy 411
south, follow US 411 for approximately 15 miles (from Madison-
ville 10 miles) to Hwy 360/Citico Road to 1st left at Fort Loudoun
Road to park visitor center.

Park Description:

Visiting Fort Loudoun Park feels like visiting four parks in one—as the park offers four unique historic sites to explore. On entering the area, the first stop should be the visitor center at the end of Fort Loudoun Road, which begins on the left after crossing Tellico Lake. The road winds through scenic woods and fields, passing a picnic area with tables and a covered pavilion, before dead-ending at a parking area near the center.

The visitor center contains a small bookstore, gift shop and museum area. Be sure to pick up brochures and a map of the park and take time to see the award-winning video film *Fort Loudoun: Forsaken By God And Man* about the history of the fort. The video brings to life the story of Fort Loudoun, which was originally built in 1756 to counter the threat of French activity during the French and Indian War.

A door from the back of the visitor center leads down a walkway to the fort, which spreads over the hillside with breathtaking views of the beautiful Tellico Lake. Within the fenced fort—with a British flag flying on the flagpole overhead—are barracks, officers' quarters, a powder magazine, bastions with cannons, a commissary storehouse, a blacksmith and tinsmith shop, a guardhouse, and many other interesting structures. It is a huge, impressive fort and fun to explore.

One of the park's nice walking trails, the Ridgetop Loop Trail (1.5 mi.) begins off the walkway near the fort. Fort Loudoun has five miles of comfortable, moderate trails. A second trail, the Meadow Loop Trail (3.3 mi.), begins out of the picnic area with a connecting pathway called the Lost Shoe Trail (0.5 mi.) off the back end of it. All the trails are easy to walk and well-maintained.

Near the visitor center and picnic area is a long fifty-foot fishing pier stretching out into the Tellico Lake. Across the road is another pull-up pier where boats can dock, making the park accessible for watercraft. Kayaking and other recreational boating is popular for visitors with so much waterfront accessible around the peninsula grounds.

Returning down Fort Loudoun Road to Hwy 360 leads to the next point in this historic park—the Sequoyah Birthplace Museum. Sequoyah, the son of a Cherokee chief's daughter and a Virginia fur trader, was a silversmith and fought with other Cherokee under General Andrew Jackson in the War of 1812. Sequoyah created a writing system for the Cherokee language which was established in 1821 and brought literacy to the Cherokee people. Sequoyah's birthplace lies less than a half-mile from the museum and village that commemorates him.

The museum covers the life of Sequoyah and the development of the alphabet. Around the grounds of the museum are a Cherokee memorial, recreated buildings, and the tent framework of

a Cherokee council house which when covered in past with bark, thatch, and other materials would seat up to 500 council members. Also on the grounds is an amphitheater where scheduled attractions, including the annual Cherokee Fall Festival in September, are presented. Some of the entertainments included in the festival are battle re-enactments, living history demonstrations, Native American dancing, and storytelling.

Past the Sequoyah Museum and across the river, a left turn leads back to the old McGhee Carson House Ruins and cemetery on a peninsula that juts out into Tellico Lake. The abandoned piece of farmland, where no one has lived for over 40 years, makes an interesting spot to visit. Park in the pull-over gravel area on the right where the McGhee Carson Road ends abruptly and walk down the continuing roadway to the cemetery and house ruins. There is no park signage to identify the start of the walk or provide the mileage to the ruins or cemetery, but walking directly down the road will lead to a trail to the old plantation ruins on the left. We did not walk to the cemetery but we did easily find the rock walls marking the entry to the old plantation house with hedgerows still lining the driveway. On the homesite we discovered old crumbling chimneys and walls, machinery relics, fencing, and other remains of the home that once stood here.

The McGhee Carson Ruins—noted as the McGhee Carson Peninsula State Historic Park on one satellite map—are named for two early owners of the land. After the government bought the Overhill territory from the Cherokee, including this land, a pioneer named John McGhee purchased what is now the ruins site and several thousand acres to develop plantations. In later generations, John Carson bought the land to farm tobacco before TVA purchased the

property for the Tellico Dam reservoir. When the dam was completed and the area flooded, this higher peninsula site, where the plantation ruins now lie, remained above water although many other nearby lands and structures were forever buried. We found it interesting to explore this old area and to imagine what life was like here for the early settlers.

Across Tellico Lake from the McGhee Carson ruins and Fort Loudoun also lie the ruins of the Tellico Blockhouse. U.S. troops were garrisoned at the blockhouse between 1794 and 1807 and several important treaties were signed between the U.S. government and the Cherokee here. To see the blockhouse ruins, return to Hwy 411 and head east, turning right on old Hwy 72 and then right again at the blockhouse signs. A paved pathway from the parking area leads down to the blockhouse remains and informative signs tell the history of events that happened on the site.

After visiting the entire park, it is easy to see why an article published on the *Only In Your State* national website cited Fort Loudoun State Historic area as one of the 15 most gorgeous state parks in Tennessee.

History Note:

Fort Loudoun was built in 1756 in the British Colonial Era to help gain Cherokee support for the British against the French. The Cherokee agreed to provide help to the British if they would construct a fort to protect their families while the men were away at war. With the new fort measuring 100 feet on each side, Fort Loudoun was larger and more elaborate than most frontier forts of its time. The structure was designed by a German-born architect named John De Brahm, who also argued for the fort's site with a commanding view of the river. When the fort was later recreated, care was taken to retain the original design. The fort was also designated a National Historic Landmark in 1965.

Indian Mountain State Park

East Tennessee - Campbell County
Park Address: 143 Indian Mtn State Park Circle, Jellico, TN 37762
Park Size: 203 Acres   Month Visited: September
Directions: From I-75 North, take exit 160 on US Hwy 25W, continuing on State Hwy 297 (S.Main) directly into Jellico and follow sgns to the park, turning right on London and left on Dairy Street, which will lead to the entrance of the park.

Park Description:

Indian Mountain State Park lies west of Jellico, just off I-75 in the Elk Valley at the base of Indian Mountain. Behind the park the mountain rises up to a summit of 1,949 feet. The north boundary forms the Kentucky-Tennessee line between the two states. Indian Mountain State Park is dominated by Indian Mountain Lake, which spreads over six acres in the middle of the park with the mountains rising behind it, creating a very scenic and picturesque site. Within the area's boundaries are a campground, picnic tables, several playgrounds, and a boathouse with rental pedal boats. Elk Creek winds its way through the park and there are several ponds and small lakes on the grounds, which are stocked for fishing with catfish, crappie, bluegill and largemouth bass.

The small town of Jellico is close by. Jellico's name came from the angelica root found readily in the area, which early settlers used to create an intoxicating brew they called "jelca" or "gelca." This plant looked somewhat like wild celery. Because this plant also had healing properties, medicines were made from it by early settlers. Many interesting plants and animals can be seen around the ponds and lakes in the park, especially on the scenic woodland walking trails. Ballard Lake Nature Trail winds in a 0.75 mile loop around Ballard Lake on the east side of the park, while the Indian Mountain Loop Trail, a paved walkway, winds for a mile along the boundary of Indian Mountain Lake. A couple of other short trails can be found in the park, but these are the two main trails.

There is a visitor center at the entry to Indian Mountain where visitors can pick up a helpful map and other information. Within the park are a boathouse and camp store near the boat dock, where pedal boats can be rented, and a bathhouse

and bathrooms near the entrance to the campground area. Indian Mountain State Park has 49 campsites for either RV or tent camping along a shady loop road. Scattered around the property are several picnic areas and three picnic shelters, and behind the lake is a swimming pool, open in the summer months. Geese and ducks enjoy the lake and all ages like the easy walking trails and the beauty of the lake and the mountains.

History Note:

In the early 1800s, coal was discovered on Jellico Mountain. Mines soon opened and Campbell County became the largest coal producer in Tennessee. In the 1940s-1950s, underground mining was replaced by surface mining in the Jellico Mountain area and a large surface mining company operated on what is now Indian Mountain State Park. In 1960, after the coal played out and the mine was abandoned, the city of Jellico, with the help of federal and state agencies, bought the property and began to restore it to create Indian Mountain State Park. This was one of the first areas in the Southeast to reclaim a strip mine area and to turn land desolated by mining back into something beautiful.

Cove Lake State Park

East Tennessee - Campbell County
Park Address: 110 Cove Lake Lane, Caryville, TN 37714
Park Size: 717 Acres   Month Visited: September
Directions: From I-75 North, take exit 134 on US Hwy 25W toward Jacksboro and LaFollette. The park entrance is on the left just past the interstate exit.

Park Description:

Cove Lake State Park spreads across a scenic valley in the Cumberland Mountains of upper East Tennessee. The park is centered around the 120 acre

Cove Lake and the waterways leading into it. Birdwatchers enjoy spotting a large variety of birds year round that make their home around the lake and woodlands, and the lake draws migratory and wintering birds and waterfowl like Canadian Geese, Great Blue Herons, and Hooded Mergansers.

Within the main part of the park grounds is a large campground with 106 campsites with water and electrical hookups, bathrooms, and a dump station. A boat dock sits on Dog Creek below the campground, where rowboats and pedal boats can be rented, and fishing is allowed along the banks of the lake. A large Olympic-sized swimming pool sits on the hillside above the campground with a nice children's playground nearby—and another alongside Cove Lake. Across from the main park on Queener Road is a public boat ramp with access to Norris Lake for recreational boating and lake fishing.

Six picnic pavilions can be found around Cove Lake and overlooking Dog Creek and over one hundred picnic tables are scattered throughout the park, many with lovely lake views. Other amenities include tennis and badminton courts, shuffleboard, horseshoes, areas for volleyball and other outdoor games.

Several walking trails wind around the lake and into the woods. We hiked the

1.4 miles Wood Loop Trail north of the lake, the loop trail around Cove Lake, and a pathway winding along the banks of Dog Creek by the boat dock. A point of interest on the north end of the lake is the Wildlife Observation Structure, a great place for viewing birds and wildlife on the lake. Across the main highway, the Cove Lake Dam can be accessed by a short 0.24 mile hike or by a trail from Twin Cove Road and Yokum Circle.

Many weddings, meetings, family reunions, and special events are held at Cove Lake. The park also offers a large indoor pavilion with a full kitchen that can accommodate up to 130 people, and next door to the indoor pavilion is the Rickard Ridge BBQ Restaurant, which also hosts buffets and events. Both the pavilion and the restaurant have panoramic views across the mountains and Cove Lake from their back windows and outdoor patios.

History Note.

Cove Lake State Park is one of the access points to the Justin P. Wilson Cumberland Trail. From the walking loop near Shelter #1 at the back of the park, hikers can access the Cumberland Trail, via the 1.0 mile

Beaver's Workshop Trail and the 1.4 miles Volunteer Loop Trail, and then climb to Bruce Creek Falls or to see the spectacular views from a rocky outcropping called the Devils Racetrack Overlook. A walking trail map and information about the park trails—and the Cumberland Trail—can be picked up in the visitor center. The 300 miles long Cumberland Trail, still under construction in many areas, will link eleven Tennessee counties from the Cumberland Gap at Kentucky's border to the Georgia border below Chattanooga. In the summer months, park rangers lead interpretive hikes to the falls and to the Devils Racetrack Overlook.

Seven Islands State Birding Park

East Tennessee - Sevier County
Park Address: 2809 Kelly Lane, Kodak, TN 37764
Park Size: 416 Acres   Month Visited: September
Directions: From I-40 East, take exit 402 Midway Road (toward River Islands Golf Club) and follow signs to the park, turning right at the white Bethel Church on Kelly Lane, which dead ends at the park gate with parking on the right.

Park Description:

Seven Islands State Birding Park is one of Tennessee's newest attractions, becoming a state park in September 2013 with its grand opening held July 1, 2014. Seven Islands' main property is located on a peninsula reaching out into the French Broad River. The tract is a wildlife refuge for songbirds, hawks, and waterfowl, and several old barns on the property provide homes for barn owls. The park is mainly river bottom land, with wide fields of tall grasses and flowers, many planted to attract native birds, insects, and pollinators. Woodlands also nestle around the rolling hills of the rural acreage and walking trails lattice the area, many originally old farm roads and others created so visitors can see the land more readily.

Many varieties of wildflowers grow in the fields, marsh, and along the trails in the park, often in sweeps as far as the eye can see. From certain high points, views of the nearby Smoky Mountains can be spotted beyond the smaller hills and ridges around the park. The birding property also includes several islands in the French Broad, and a parcel of land across the river, where Mutton Hollow Landing provides access to the river for boating and fishing. Near the entrance of the park off Kelly Lane, a side roadway leads down to a second boat launch, Seven Islands Landing, with access for small boats, canoes, and kayaks.

As a new facility, Seven Islands Park does not have typical amenities, like camping or playground facilities, or even a visitor center or bathrooms yet, although there is a porta-potty near the main parking area. Visitors will also find picnic tables in the barn beside the parking area and a few more a short distance down the Seclusion Trail near the Seven Islands Landing.

Besides the hundreds of native birds that live year round in Seven Islands, the park is on the migratory path for other birds, as well. More than 180 species have been sighted and identified, and many research studies and educational programs are ongoing at the park, including bird banding and mapping by bird biologists and trained volunteers. On designated days visitors can come to watch the banding and learn more about the wildlife of the area. Birds are best seen in morning and late evening, so visitors may not see many birds in the midday hours.

Around the park property are eight miles of scenic trails. We walked the 1.23 miles paved Kelly Lane Greenway by the Kelly farmstead and rustic barn and on to the end of the peninsula. Next we explored the 2.67 miles Seclusion Bend Trail along the French Broad River and hiked around the 1.33 miles Seven Island Loop Trail. This pathway travels by Wayne's Pond, into the woods and then back through native grass fields dotted with bluebird houses to return again to the parking area.

History Note.

The property now occupied by the park used to belong to the Kelly and Creswell families. The Kellys owned and farmed the bulk of the property on the north end of Seven Islands. The Creswells owned the land on the south end of the peninsula, where they farmed and operated a sand-dredging company. Descendants of both families still live in the East Tennessee area.

Norris Dam State Park

East Tennessee - Anderson/Campbell County
Park Address: 125 Village Green Circle, Rocky Top, TN 37769
Park Size: 4,000 Acres   Month Visited: September
Directions: From I-75 take exit 128 and go 2.5 miles south on
Hwy 441 to the entrance of the park on the west end or to enter the
east end, take exit 122 onto TN-61 E and turn left onto Hwy 441 at
park sign after the Museum of Appalachia.

Park Description:

Norris Dam State Park covers a vast acreage of land on either side of the
dam along the shorelines of Norris Lake. The park, diverse in topography, offers
a wide variety of amenities—picnic areas, camping grounds, cabin rentals, recreational areas, a swimming pool, a deluxe marina, historic structures, and many
hiking trails.

The park has two distinct sections, the East Park on the eastern side
of Norris Dam and the West Park on the western side. Entering from the east
end will bring visitors into the older developed area of the state park, where its
historic structures lie. On Hwy 441, in a wedge of land amid the TVA managed
property below the dam, lies the Lenoir Museum Cultural Complex. Here visitors will find the Lenoir Museum, the Caleb Crosby Threshing Barn, and the 18th
Century Rice Grist Mill, all situated on a scenic area along Lower Clear Creek.
The threshing barn, originally built in the 1830s, was saved from flooding by the
Norris Lake reservoir and later reassembled on the park site. Near the barn is the

historic Rice Grist Mill. It was originally constructed in 1798 in another nearby area scheduled for flooding, and the Civilian Conservation Corps (CCC) and the National Park Service disassembled the mill and moved it to the present site. During the summer, the water wheel is still operated and visitors can buy cornmeal inside the gristmill gift shop. A short walk from the mill sits the Lenoir Museum, which contains Will and Helen Lenoir's collection of historic artifacts donated to the park. In the museum are displays of early American farm implements, furniture, china, tools, an antique barrel organ, and more. Tours are available in the museum by request.

Continuing up the east end of Hwy 441 leads to the main entrance to the east side of the Norris Dam State Park, marked by a large entry sign. Twining around the road to the right leads visitors to fine picnic grounds on the hillsides with several large pavilions for rental. The east side campground has 25 sites with water, electric hookups, a bathhouse, and dump station as well as ten more primitive campsites down a winding back road for tent camping. A charming aspect of the east campground area are the 19 historic cabins sitting around a quiet wooded loop road. These were built by the CCC in the 1930s and the rockwork on many is really beautiful. The old rustic Tea Room can be found near the cabin area, which can be rented for group events. Across from the Tea Room is a big playground and an outdoor amphitheater, and behind the Tea Room is an access path to the CCC Trails System on the east side of the park.

After leaving the east section and driving across Norris Dam, visitors

Norris Dam State Park:

- Visitor Center * Cabins * Swimming * Picnic Pavilions
* Playgrounds * Fishing * Camping - RV Sites * Hiking/Biking Trails
* Marina * Boat Rentals * Boat Launch Ramp * Museum
* Planned Programs * Gift Shop * Tennis Courts * Water Skiing

will find a full size marina behind the dam. Norris Dam Marina has a fine boat ramp and boat rentals, including kayak, canoe, paddleboard, ski-boat, pontoon, and houseboat rentals, a store selling bait and fishing tackle, and a restaurant with indoor and outdoor dining. On a hillside above the marina, on TVA property, is a fine overlook with views out across the marina, dam, lake and Clinch River. Continuing west on Hwy 441 leads into the western part of the park. Village Green Road leads up to a picnic area and the main visitor center complex with a gift shop, large swimming pool, recreation hall, tennis and basketball courts, and a playground. Beyond the Village Green recreation area lie the deluxe AAA cabin rentals, newer units with several bedrooms, gas fireplaces, central heat and air, and more modern amenities than the rustic cabins.

Continuing into the far western section on Andrews Ridge Road leads to the second campground with 50 camping sites with full facilities for RV and tent camping. This is a beautiful and popular campground on a wooded hillside loop road with its own dump station and bathhouse. We saw many large RV coaches parked in this popular scenic area. A boat ramp can be found on an inlet of the lake on the road connecting the two park areas.

A hallmark of the Norris Dam State Park is its 21 miles of wooded hiking trails scattered throughout the east and west sections of the property. On the east side of the park visitors can attain easy access to the Lakeside Trail near the dam

and the Lakeside Loop, Christmas Fern Trail, and the Tall Timbers Trail beginning near the Tea Room. Our favorite trails lay on the west side of the park, all broad, easy to walk woods trails stretching out from the recreation and west campground areas. We walked portions of the Marine Railway Loop and the Harmon Loop, and farther west in the park we hiked the Andrews Ridge Trail, Hootin' Hollow Trail, part of the Rock Creek Trail, and the Sinkhole Loop Trail. All are well-maintained and provide comfortable walks for all ages.

Norris Dam State Park has many ongoing interpretive programs and events year round for visitors to enjoy like Pickin' in the Park Concerts, Fall Color Boat Trips, guided hikes, history tours including Lenoir Museum and Rice Grist Mill Tours, story events, special children's events in summer, and other seasonal activities. It's a great park to visit at any time of year.

History Note.

Norris Dam was the first dam created by the Tennessee Valley Authority (TVA), formed as a part of Franklin D. Roosevelt's New Deal legislation. The land lying closely around and below the dam, sandwiched between the east and west sections of the state park, is still controlled and managed by the TVA. Norris Dam, a large hydroelectric dam, is 1,860 feet long and 265 feet high. To build the dam and its reservoir a total of 152,000 acres of land was attained, displacing nearly 3,000 families and causing the relocation of over 5,000 graves. Some historic structures were saved, moved, and stand inside the park grounds today. Below the dam, a popular 2.3 miles walking loop, called the Songbird Trail, is enjoyed by locals of the area, as is the River Bluff Trail on the west side of the Clinch River. Anglers also enjoy fishing the Clinch River tailwater below the dam for trout. A visitor center by the dam is staffed by TVA retirees.

Hiwassee/Ocoee Rivers State Park

East Tennessee - Polk County
Park Address: 404 Spring Creek Road, Delano, TN 37325
Park Size: 23 miles managed river section
Month Visited: October
Directions: Follow Hwy 411 south through Etowah, past Delano, and turn on Spring Creek Road to reach park headquarters and Gee Creek Campground.

Park Description:

The main facility of the Hiwassee and Ocoee Rivers State Park is more of a central hub for a recreational area than a typical state park contained in a designated acreage. The full park property actually contains 23 miles of river sections of the Hiwassee River and Ocoee River known the world over for white water rafting. The 1996 Olympic Slalom Course events were held on the Ocoee, bringing the region international attention.

The park's white water river sections are divided into three main regions, one on the Hiwassee River and two on the Ocoee. Most sections on the Hiwassee are Class I and II, with a few Class III spots requiring more skill and maneuvering. The Middle Ocoee region offers varied class experiences, while the Upper Ocoee, where the Olympic Whitewater events were held, goes from Class II to Class IV and is restricted to age 12 and older. Several rafting outfitters provide rafts and guides, kayaks, and tubes, and there are also launch sites for those with their own equipment at public and private launch sites along the rivers.

The Gee Creek park section, that includes the visitor center, camping and picnic grounds, lies on Spring Creek Road. At the visitor center tourists can attain information about the area and pick up helpful maps and brochures. Behind the visitor center is the Fort Marr Blockhouse, the only remaining structure of the 1800s Fort Marr that was originally built on Old Federal Road

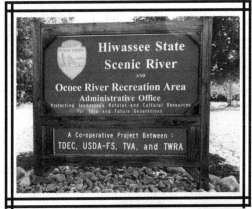

and later moved to the Hiwassee/Ocoee area. The Gee Creek Campground offers 47 simple campsites in a scenic area that includes a children's park, picnic tables, and a winding, scenic walking path called the Gee Creek Trail. We walked this mile long trail section and enjoyed it. An access road leads to an outdoor theatre for park events and to a paved boat launch on the Hiwassee River. Fishing is popular on the river, stocked by TWRA, and anglers catch bass, perch, catfish, and trout.

Adjacent to the park and Gee Creek Campground is the 2,500 acres Gee Creek Wilderness area that lies between Starr and Chestnut mountains. Parts of the John Muir Trail, Benton McKay Trail, and many other scenic hiking trails can be found in this area. The park office provides information about the Wilderness area and directions for a short hike to Gee Creek Falls, a 25 foot falls on the nearby Gee Creek.

The railway for the Hiwassee River Rail Adventure lies across the street from the park headquarters and campground. We enjoyed watching a crowd of visitors load onto the historic 1950s train for one of its 3.5-hour excursion runs. Riders taking the "Hiwassee Loop" excursion or the longer "Copperhill Special" are taken by bus from the Etowah train depot to the loading area across from the Gee Creek Ranger Station.

Red Clay State Historic Park

East Tennessee - Bradley County
Park Address: 1140 Red Clay Park Rd, Cleveland, TN 37311
Park Size: 263 acres   Month Visited: October
Directions: Follow I-75 south of Cleveland, turn on Hwy 74 by-pass loop and take Blue Springs Road Exit south and follow signs to Park.

Park Description:

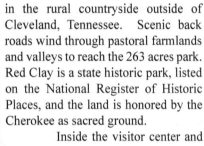

The Red Clay State Park lies in the rural countryside outside of Cleveland, Tennessee. Scenic back roads wind through pastoral farmlands and valleys to reach the 263 acres park. Red Clay is a state historic park, listed on the National Register of Historic Places, and the land is honored by the Cherokee as sacred ground.

Inside the visitor center and gift shop at Red Clay, visitors can learn about Cherokee history and see artifacts on display. In the center, named the James F. Corn Interpretive Facility, there is also a video theater, a small library, and a room of interesting exhibits. Often workshops and programs are held for visitors and school groups in the theater. Several well-known annual events and Pow Wows are held at Red Clay every year—the Red Clay Homecoming in March, craft fairs in May and September, Cherokee Days of Recognition in October, and the Trail of Lights Christmas Celebration in December. Tents and structures were being set up for the October Red Clay Pow Wow when we visited. The annual weekend event offers an opportunity to see Native American tribes from across the nation, to enjoy tribal dancing and music, to hear stories and to visit historical sites and craft booths.

It was at Red Clay where the Cherokee people came together to have their "councils" or meetings from 1832 until 1838, before they had to leave their lands. Councils often lasted several weeks and eleven councils were held at Red Clay as the Cherokee people struggled to hold on to their lands and not be evicted. After the Cherokee left the Red Clay area all existing structures were torn down and the government sold the land to farmers. However, in 1979, the state of Tennessee bought the land and created a state historic park. Structures were then built to represent the former buildings—a council house, Cherokee farm cabins, barns, and other outbuildings.

Visitors to the park can walk through the historic village to see what life was like for the Indians when Red Clay was the Cherokee capital. A new addition to the park is a group of mask carvings of the seven Cherokee clans that were created from the stumps of old trees by Cherokee artist John Grant. An interpretive trail passes the masks and leads around the historic area of the park. On a hillside overlooking the village is the rock monument called

51

The Eternal Flame. The fire in this monument is always kept burning as a memorial to all who suffered and died on the Trail of Tears.

Visitors to Red Clay can also see the Blue Hole Spring, a natural landmark. This unique spring rises from under a limestone ledge to pool out into Mill Creek. The pool has a distinctive blue hue—especially pretty in the sunlight. A scenic pathway winds down to the Blue Hole and to a bridge across the creek. The spring provided water for the Indians during their council meetings and both the spring and pool are sacred to the Cherokee. Above Mill Creek and the Blue Hole Spring, the short Blue Hole nature trail begins, moving down a shady lane to later wind into the woods.

On the right side of the Red Clay Park, a side road curls around to a pretty picnic area with a large covered pavilion on the hill above it. Near the pavilion is a giant outdoor amphitheater, seating up to 500 people, where many of the park's events are held. Behind the amphitheater is a pathway leading into the Council of Trees Trail. Starting at this point, we walked the 1.7 miles loop trail as it wound its way through the woods and up to a ridge top. It then moved downhill on the other side to come out behind the picnic pavilion, passing many large rock structures along the way. At the top of the ridge, the trail opens out to reach the Overlook Tower, a giant limestone structure right in the middle of the forest. It's an incredible sight rising two stories high with a sweeping flight of rock steps winding gracefully up to it! Surprisingly, no explanatory plaques tell who built the Overlook Tower, when, how, or for what reason. From the top of the tower, you can walk around and enjoy vistas out across the surrounding forest although the trees obscure any distant views. We thought this tower was one of the park's

highlights and visitors can walk to the tower from either end of the loop.

This small park was packed with interesting sights to see, and visitors will learn a lot about the Cherokee while visiting this historic site.

History Note:

All the land at Red Clay was once owned by the Cherokee. In an earlier time, the Cherokee tribe controlled a large part of the southeastern United States, but their lands were gradually sold off or taken. Despite earlier altercations, Cherokee Indians had lived peaceably with the white settlers since the 1700s. They had become farmers, adopted white ways, and even fought with the Tennessee militia and US army in critical battles. They believed they would be allowed to stay on their remaining lands in southeast Tennessee, north Georgia, Alabama, and southwestern North Carolina, but two pieces of legislation changed their hopes.

In 1830, during the presidency of Andrew Jackson, the Indian Removal Act passed, authorizing the government to negotiate with southeastern Indian tribes to exchange their southern lands for territory west of the Mississippi. Then in 1835 the Treaty of Echota was signed between a group of Cherokee leaders and the U.S. Government ceding all their lands east of the Mississippi to the government, with an agreement to move west to Indian Territory. The Cherokee

received new homeland territory in Oklahoma and five million dollars in this treaty. However, the treaty was not approved by the whole Cherokee National Council or signed by its chief at the time. A difficult period for the Cherokee ensued as they tried to appeal the treaty, but to no avail. Most Cherokee believed they would still not be forced to leave their lands. However, in 1838, the enforcement of the Indian Removal Act began and the military started to force the Cherokee from their homelands, initiating the Trail of Tears. It was a dark time in American history, and thousands of Cherokee people lost their lives during the forced journey to Oklahoma.

Frozen Head State Park & Natural Area

East Tennessee - Morgan County
Park Address: 964 Flat Fork Road, Wartburg, TN 37887
Park Size: 24,000 acres   Month Visited: December
Directions: From Harriman, take Hwy 27N to Wartburg, turn right
on Hwy 62. Travel 2 miles and turn left on Flat Fork Road for 4
miles, to park entrance on right. From Knoxville, take Pellissippi
Pkwy toward Oak Ridge. Stay on Hwy 62 to Oliver Springs and
toward Wartburg. Turn right on Flat Fork Rd and to park entrance.

Park Description:

Frozen Head State Park is located in
the Crab Orchard Mountains west of Walden
Ridge in the southern end of the Cumberland
Mountain Range. The park is centered along
Flat Fork Valley between Bird Mountain and
Old Mac Mountain. Frozen Head, the highest mountain that the park is named for, rises
near the center of the park to 3,324 feet and is
often covered with snow and ice in the winter months. In 1988 the majority of the park
was designated as a state natural area, except
for the 330 acres where the main park headquarters and campgrounds are located. As a
natural area, the park is known for its beautiful forests, mountains, wildflowers, birding,
fishing, and hiking trails.

After entering the park, visitors
come to the visitor center with a gift shop,
nice restrooms, and a picnic area across the
street by the stream. Fishing is popular in
Frozen Head along Flat Fork Creek as it is
stocked with rainbow trout. Behind the
visitor center, The Chimney Top Trail winds
steeply uphill on rocky steps to begin its 6.3
miles climb to the rocky bluffs and overlook
on Chimney Top Mountain. A little further
up the road beyond the visitor center and
ranger residence is a playground and picnic
area with access to several other hiking trails. The Old Mac Trail leads out of
the back of the parking lot, soon intersecting the Interpretive Trail Loop and the
South Old Mac Trail (2.7 miles), which climbs to Old Mac Mountain at 3,132

feet. Judge Branch Trail (1.2 miles), Spicewood Trail (2.5 miles), and the North Old Mac Trail (3.6 miles) are also accessed from this parking area.

We especially enjoyed our hike along the Interpretive Trail Loop and the Spicewood Trail that took us by the remnants of an old Civilian Conservation Corps (CCC) Camp. From 1933 to 1941 at the onset of World War II, CCCs maintained a camp here along Spicewood Branch. The CCC workers shaped many of the park's structures and trails, created rock walls and the ranger's headquarters, and built the fire tower at the summit on Frozen Head. Remnants of the CCC camp can be found all along the trail—old cisterns, moss-covered chimneys, the foundations of structures and buildings—and on the South Old Mac Trail a CCC dynamite camp shack. Often the rangers lead interpretive tours telling visitors about the CCC history and in the summer the CCCs hold an all-day reunion at the park.

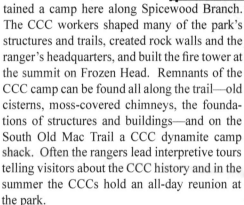

Continuing up the main road leads to more picnic areas, two more shelters and the park's main campground. Almost parallel to the road, the Flat Fork Nature Trail winds through the woods and along the stream, an easy, lightly graveled 0.4 mile trail, suitable for strollers, young children, and bicycling. A bridge across Flat Fork Creek leads to another pavilion and a playground in a scenic spot with an arching bridge beside it. Down a short trail from the pavilion lies a large outdoor amphitheater, seating 240, where many events are held in the summer months. As in many state parks, the campground is closed and gated November 1st to March 15th, but in-season there are ample campsites available, each with grills and a picnic table, and a shared bathhouse. Other rustic campsites and two group camping areas

are scattered throughout the park as well. At the back of the campground area a trail called the Bird Mountain Trail (4.3 miles) climbs up to Bird Mountain, Castle Rock, and loops into the North Bird Mountain Trail (5.5 miles). In addition, the 6.2 miles Lookout Tower Trail, originally a logging road, climbs out of the back of the campground to rise to the top of Frozen Head Mountain. Mountain bikers can also ride up this unpaved road to the tower. Frozen Head is one of the highest peaks west of the Smoky Mountains and on a clear day you can see the Smokies peaks from the 360 degrees observation deck on the fire tower.

At the end of Flat Fork Road is a trailhead parking area for several more trails before the road loops to head back out of the park. We hiked three popular trails in this area to DeBord Falls, to Emory Gap Falls, and along Panther Branch Trail. From out of the parking area an open roadbed trail, called Emory Gap Trail, winds in a gradual ascent along Flat Fork Creek into the mountain. The stream, reminiscent of rushing mountain streams in the Smoky Mountains, offers views and access points to many cascades and swimming holes. At one half mile up the trail, a side pathway with stairs and a handrail, leads down to the base of beautiful DeBord Falls, a 12-foot plunge waterfall on Panther Branch. Continuing another half-mile up Emory Gap Trail leads to the intersection of the Panther Branch Trail. The 2.3 miles trail begins by crossing Flat Fork Creek on a log bridge, then follows along Panther Branch to eventually cross the creek and intersect the North Old Mac Trail.

After exploring DeBord Falls and some of the Panther Branch Trail, we returned to the Emory Gap Trail to hike another 0.6 mile to a second waterfall called Emory Gap Falls. Steeper than the earlier trail, this path narrows to wind up

and over a ridge top to the 25 foot plunge waterfall on Bird Mountain at the head-waters of Flat Fork Creek. The path down to the falls requires some climbing and clambering over rocks and logs to get close to the long cascade spilling over a rocky ledge.

The portion of the park we explored is only one primary area of the full park acreage. It would take several visits to hike all the park's many trails. In spring the park is known for its vast variety of wild-flowers, and at the visitor center guests can pick up an extensive checklist of wild-flowers to look for. The park also hosts Wildflower Pilgrimages in April on the 2nd and 3rd weekends with guided tours to see the park's flowers.

History Note.

Frozen Head State Park adjoins the property of the old Brushy Mountain State Prison. The state of Tennessee bought a large tract of wilderness land in Morgan County and the prison opened in 1896. The maximum-security prison, looking like a medieval fortress, lay surrounded by the Walden Ridge Mountains. Prisoners helped to build the prison from natural resources in the

area, worked on the land, and in the prison's coal mines. Several trails in Frozen Head, like the Old Prison Mine Trail, lead to areas once used by the facility. Remotely located in a wilderness valley, no prisoners ever escaped Brushy Mountain without being caught. In 2009, the prison was closed and in January 2015 the state gave Brushy Mountain back to Morgan County. Plans are now underway to create a campground, RV park, stables, walking trails, a restaurant, B & B, bottled water facility, distillery, and a museum on the old prison grounds.

Harrison Bay State Park

East Tennessee - Hamilton County
Park Address: 8411 Harrison Bay Rd, Harrison, TN 37341
Park Size: 1,200 acres   Month Visited: February
Directions: From I-75, take one of these routes over to Hwy 58:
(1) coming from the south, above Chattanooga, take Hwy 153 to
travel north on Hwy 58 or (2) coming from the north, take Hwy
312 at the Cleveland exit and travel west to Hwy 58. Then follow
Hwy 58 to Harrison Bay Road and to the park entrance sign.

Park Description:

Harrison Bay State Park is a
1,200 acres park sprawling for miles
along the Chickamauga Lake. At the
park entrance is a small brown building utilized as a nature center office.
Drive past the nature center and swing
left, following the signs to the main
visitor center and park office in the
big red-roofed building by the marina.
Inside you can pick up informational
pieces about the area, a park brochure
and map. The Dockside Restaurant is
located next door and in season you
can enjoy meals inside or out on the
deck with fine views across the lake.

Behind the park office is Harrison Bay's extensive marina. It offers
161 covered slips, 28 uncovered slips
and four sailboat slips, available for
monthly or yearly rental, and it can
accommodate boats up to 60 feet. In
the warmer seasons kayaks, canoes,
and paddleboards can be rented, and
the marina sells ice, snacks, and gas.
There is a fine public boat launch ramp
right by the marina – one of two in the
park. The other ramp is at the Wolfte-
ver location off Highway 58. During
the summer months the lake buzzes
with boating enthusiasts enjoying the
beautiful stretches of accessible lake.

Near the Marina is the trailhead for one of three walking trails in the park. The Bay Point Loop Trail circles the park for 4.5 miles through the woods and along the sides of the lake with markers and benches along the way. A moderate trail, it is very popular with walkers and bikers—and dogs can walk on leash on the trail. Closer to the park entrance is the Harrison Bay Walking Trail, a shorter 0.5 mile loop trail weaving through a wooded and grassy area known for butterflies, insects, and birds in the warmer months. Birdhouses dot the area and an observation deck has been created in the middle of the tall prairie grass for enjoying the views. A short distance up the main road from the walking trail is the Lakeshore Loop, a half-mile walking trail that winds down to the lake and back. This spot on the lake is a good place for fishing as well.

Fishing is very popular at Harrison Bay State Park with so many readily accessible shorelines, a long fishing pier, and easy access for boats. For licensed anglers fishing is excellent with bass, catfish, crappie and other fish commonly caught. In the first week of June kids can fish free all week, without a license, and on the first Saturday in June, anyone can fish free.

Camping enthusiasts love Harrison Bay, as it has 128 RV campsites with water and electrical hookups that can accommodate large RVs, along with 27 tent campsites. The campsites are spread around the park in shady, scenic areas with bathhouses, a dump station, and a cute camp store. For added pleasure there is a ball field, a playground, a recreation hall, and an Olympic-sized

Harrison Bay State Park:

• Visitor Center * Group Camp * Swimming * Picnic Pavilions
* Playgrounds * Fishing * Camping - RV Sites * Hiking/Biking Trails
* Marina * Boat Rentals * Boat Launch Ramp * Golf Course
* Restaurant (seasonal)

swimming pool at Harrison Bay. The large pool is a beautiful one with a separate pool for toddlers and non-swimmers. The park's Recreation Hall can be rented for group events, weddings, or other family activities. It has a stage, a full kitchen, and a deck that looks across the lake. Picnic tables and shelters are also scattered around the park, many with picturesque vistas out across the water.

Harrison Bay also offers a big group camp area, separate from the main park area in a pretty wooded location. The camp has 24 rustic cabins, scattered around a quiet loop road, a big dining hall, a well-equipped playground, volleyball and basketball courts, and a ball field. This would be a great area for young people in scouts, church groups, or other youth organizations, offering a private meeting area while still close to all the other amenities of the park. The group camp can accommodate up to 144 people at one time.

During the summer many family activities are offered at the park including ranger-led nature walks and talks. Bird watching is popular at Harrison Bay and many birdhouses can be seen around the property. Located along a 40-miles stretch of the Chickamauga Lake, the park is home to a wide variety of shorebirds and is visited by migratory birds. Many waterfowl winter in the area and Harrison Bay is also home to osprey and bald eagles. We walked down to the tenth hole of the golf course to see the giant eagle nest in the high crook of a pine tree near the lake's edge.

The golf course at Harrison Bay, located up the main highway a little distance from the main activities of the park, is a well-known, classic course designed by Jack Nicklaus. The course lies in an ideal setting with wooded land along its fairways with the lake never far from sight. Water touches twelve of the course's Bermuda grass fairways, which were brown at our winter visit to the park. A large practice range and putting green lie near the parking area and clubhouse. Inside the clubhouse is a golf shop, lounge area around a rustic rock fireplace, and the Bear Trace Restaurant. We ate lunch at the restaurant and enjoyed the views out the back of the clubhouse that looked over the fairways and down to the lake. The Bear Trace Gold course received the 2009 Governor's Environmental Stewardship Award for Excellence in Parks and Recreation. The course has naturalized 40 acres of the course, created a plant bed of 218 plants native to Tennessee, and installed 45 nesting houses around the golf course to encourage wildlife. The course has even been designated as a Certified Audubon Cooperative Sanctuary.

One especially nice aspect of this park is that all the amenities are clustered around winding roads along the lakeside so that visitors can easily walk or bike from one area to another. Picnic areas and campsites were situated in scenic spots under shady trees or along the shorelines with stunning views. This is a beautiful park, perfect for all ages.

History Note.

The name of Harrison Bay State Park comes from the old town of Harrison, which was covered by water when the Tennessee Valley Authority created the Chickamauga Dam and Chickamauga Lake. Nearly 8,000 people lived in the old town of Harrison that developed southeast of a ferry crossing called Vann's Crossing. The city was flooded in 1940, like scenes portrayed in the 1960 movie *Wild River*. Evidence of old roads and the foundations of old buildings can still be seen in some places around the park. Harrison was also the last Cherokee Campground, consisting of three Cherokee villages.

Booker T. Washington State Park

East Tennessee - Hamilton County
Park Address: 5801 Champion Rd, Chattanooga, TN 37416
Park Size: 353 acres   Month Visited: February
Directions: From I-75 north of Chattanooga, turn left on Hwy 153
and follow to right on Hwy 58. Turn left on Champion Road at
the park sign and follow to the state park entrance.

Park Description:

     The Booker T. Washington State Park lies close to Chattanooga, Red Bank, and Hixson in southeastern Tennessee, eight miles from the Harrison Bay State Park. It covers 353 acres in a lovely setting on the shorelines of the Chickamauga Lake. The park was named for the famous educator and statesman Booker Taliaferro Washington, who was an African American leader who wrote 14 books, was an advisor to the president, and founded the Tuskegee Institute.

     Just inside the entrance is a visitor center where you can pick up brochures, information about events and activities, and a park map. Most of the main amenities lie on a peninsula jutting into the Chickamauga Lake with scenic views of the lake at every turn. The main road into the park leads back to picnic and recreational areas beside the lake. Booker T. Washington offers a big Olympic-sized swimming pool, bathhouse, children's playground, basketball courts, horseshoe pit, and a large recreation assembly hall. After the pool area, a road to the right drops to a parking area beside the lake near a large picnic pavilion and an accessible entrance to the park's main walking and biking trail. This trail leads to a

six miles lattice of biking trails winding through the woodlands and along the shoreline of the park, a favorite area for biking enthusiasts. The trails are challenging but can be biked by all abilities. Many trail sections are also popular with hikers.

Near the main trail entrance is one of the park's boat docks and a beautiful fishing pier reaching out into the lake. Fishing is especially popular at Booker T. Washington with many fine places to fish from the banks or pier and with a boat ramp for anglers preferring fishing out on the water. Favorite catches are crappie, catfish, and bass.

Although the park does not have camping facilities for tent or RV camping, there are an abundance of picnic areas around the park and three picnic shelters available for group rentals. The park also has a beautiful group camp area called the Oaks Group Camp. Modern and recently completed in 2014, the camp has six large cabins, a beautiful dining hall, a bathhouse, outdoor play areas, a basketball court and a large covered pavilion. The Margaret Murray Washington Assembly Hall within the camp can be rented separately for special events.

Down the street from the Oaks Camp is the Booker T. Washington Group Lodge consisting of three buildings. The lodge offers barracks-style rooms, a big recreation area, a kitchen and dining area, ideal for youth groups and other civic organization use. Reservations for the camp or lodge can be made through the main office. In season, the park rangers offer guided hikes and help with events like the Spring Scavenger Hunt and Hike held in March.

Justin P. Wilson Cumberland Trail State Park

East Tennessee
Park Address: 220 Park Road, Caryville, TN 37714
(Begins in Claiborne County; ends in Hamilton County)
Park Size: 330+ miles trail   Month Visited: May
Directions: To get to the beginning of the trail, travel I-81 to the
Morristown exit to 25E. Continue on 25E through Tazewell to
Harrogate. Pass Lincoln Memorial University and turn right on
US 58 before the tunnel. Take first left on Brooklyn Street through
Cumberland Gap to the Iron Furnace parking lot at the Cumber-
land Gap National Historic Park boundary.

Park Description:

The Justin P. Wilson Cum-
berland Trail State Park is not a self-
contained park area. Instead it is a
linear tract following 330+ projected
miles of the Cumberland Trail from
the beginning, near the Kentucky border at Cumberland Gap, Tennessee,
to the end near the Georgia border
below Chattanooga, Tennessee. The
trail moves in a southwesterly journey
through eleven counties of Tennessee.
At the date of this book's publication,
the park was still a "work in progress,"
with new lands continuing to be added, such as a 1,034 acres tract around
Soak Creek in Rhea County in early
2017. As of spring 2017, 95% of the
total property for the project had been
donated or purchased, with the work to
finish the total trail construction about
65% complete.

The origins of the Cumber-
land Trail started in the 1980s, with
a group reviving the effort in the
1990s. In 1998 the ongoing trail became Tennessee's 53rd state park and
in 2002 it was renamed the Justin P.
Wilson Cumberland Trail in honor of
the Deputy Governor's vision to make
the trail a reality. Future plans are for
the Cumberland Trail to link into The

Great Eastern Trail, a north-south hiking trail still under development that will run for almost a thousand miles from New York to Alabama.

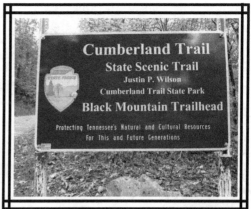

The long Cumberland Trail, at this time, is divided into twelve segments with sections in each, starting with the Cumberland Mountain Segment at the Tennessee-Kentucky border and ending at the Tennessee River Gorge Segment near the Tennessee-Georgia border. The trail begins at a point in the Cumberland Gap National Historical Park called the Tri State Peak, where the states of Virginia, Kentucky, and Tennessee meet. We hiked to this beginning point of the park from the Iron Furnace parking lot behind the small town of Cumberland Gap, Tennessee.

The early path initially leads past the Iron Furnace and then up the Tennessee Trail to intersect the Wilderness Road Trail, before turning left uphill on the Tri-State Trail leading to the peak. Total mileage to get to the Tri-State Peak from the Iron Furnace parking lot is approximately one and a half miles. The hike to the trailhead is an easy walk to follow, if somewhat steep, with gorgeous views from the Tri-State Peak pavilion down over the valley. The Cumberland park trailhead begins right behind the Tri-State Peak pavilion on top of the mountain. White painted markers on the trees mark the route, which follows the ridgeline along the top of the mountain. The first two miles of the trail are well-blazed and at approximately 1.5 miles from the trailhead, the path turns sharply right, leading to a fine overlook at two miles with

views across the Cumberland Mountains stretching to Virginia.

The Cumberland Trail next begins a journey across the high ridgetops to LaFollette, running parallel to Highway 63. This section of the trail is complete, although not all the route is easy to hike or follow. At LaFollette, access to the trail can be made at the Tank Springs Trailhead. The hike then moves into the Eagle Bluff Section, traveling over some rocky terrain before dropping down behind Cove Lake State Park to the Bruce Gap Trailhead access point. We walked some of the trail in this section along Cove Creek.

Moving southwest, the Cumberland Trail continues through the Frozen Head State Park and Natural Area and the Catoosa Wildlife Management Area to cross Interstate 40 near Ozone Falls and Crossville. We explored more of the park in this Grassy Cove Segment, which includes the Black Mountain, Brady Mountain, and Ozone Falls Sections of the Cumberland Trail, not all fully completed at this time. The state park website notes the sections of the trail completed and rates their difficulty, and the park brochure shows access points to the different segments. It also gives a link to the Cumberland Trail Guide website

where more detailed descriptions of each part of the trail are available.

Ozone Falls, near Crab Orchard, Tennessee, just off Interstate 40, is easy to get to by car, and it is only a short distance from the falls parking lot to views above and below the falls. Ozone Falls is in the Ozone Falls State Natural Area in Cumberland County about midway along the Justin P. Wilson Cumberland Trail. The falls plunges 110 feet over sandstone rock into a deep pool. The falls is on US Highway 70 about four miles east of the Crab Orchard exit. The nearby Black Mountain section of the Cumberland Trail is not far away. This completed trail section climbs through forestland and into a rocky section at the top of the mountain with giant rocks and a cave.

One pretty section that the Cumberland Trail will travel through, and make more accessible to hikers, is the Piney Falls State Natural Area near Grandview. Already accessible is a 1.6 miles trail loop that leads back to Piney Falls, an 80-foot waterfall cascading over the rocks. The trailhead starts from a parking area on Fire Tower Road and loops around to Upper Piney Falls and Lower Piney Falls before returning. The route of the Cumberland Trail passes through and by many state natural areas with falls, overlooks, rock formations, and other beautiful natural spots for hikers to enjoy.

Beyond the Piney River Segment, many trail sections behind Spring City and Dayton in the mountains near Highway 27 are not fully completed yet. Heading southwest the lower part of the Cumberland Trail moves behind the Soddy Daisy area and into the North Chickamauga Creek Gorge. Beyond yet another incomplete section, the trail enters the Prentice Cooper State Forest and Wildlife Management Area behind Chattanooga and Signal Point across the Tennessee River. Signal Point, high on Signal Mountain, was a communications station for the Union Army during the Civil War. The Signal and Edwards Points Section serves as the southern terminus of the Cumberland Trail. There are multiple overlooks of the Tennessee River Gorge here. This southern end of the trail is accessible from US Hwy 127 from the paved parking area for Signal Point. A paved pathway leads 360 feet to an overlook with a panoramic view of the Tennessee River Gorge. At 0.4 mile you can see 90-foot Julia Falls and at approximately one mile, you can view Rainbow Falls below the trail on the left. At the publication of this guidebook no official visitor center has opened at any of the access points of the Justin P. Wilson Cumberland Trail.

Rocky Fork State Park

East Tennessee - Unicoi County
Park Address: 501 Rocky Fork Rd, Flag Pond, TN 37657
Park Size: 2,037 acres   Month Visited: August
Directions: From I-81, travel I-26E through Johnson City and Erwin to Exit 43. Turn left at end of exit ramp and then right on US 19W following park signs. Stay right onto Hwy 352/Temple Hills Road to Rocky Fork Road and park entrance on right. Follow Rocky Fork approximately 1 mile to main parking area on left.

Park Description:

Rocky Fork State Park is one of the newest in the park system, added in 2012. It covers a beautiful sweep of wilderness in the southern Appalachian Mountains with the Cherokee National Forest bordering three sides of the park acreage. At the publication date of this guidebook, the park did not yet have completed facilities or amenities, although a ranger station and visitor center are planned for future development. Fishing is allowed in Rocky Fork and in South Indian Creek as well as downstream near the main entrance gate, but check with the park service about fishing regulations.

The area is a paradise for hikers with a broad network of trails weaving through the park's mountainous terrain and alongside clear sparkling streams. Many of the trails were once logging and wildlife management roads and these gravel or dirt roads are wide enough for several hikers to walk side by side on. Trails on the southwest end of the park lead to an access point to the Appalachian Trail at Flint Gap. A detailed map, showing the hiking trails in Rocky Fork, is available on the state park website, and it is helpful to download and print this map before planning a trip to explore the park. Camping or campfires are not allowed at this time in Rocky Fork so explorations should be daytime ventures, returning before dark.

On our visit to the park, we hiked from the main parking area up Rocky Fork Trail along the tumbling Rocky Fork stream, with its rushing cascades, waterfalls, and pools. We stopped at Black Stack Falls, Triple Falls, and several other scenic points for photo shoots and to walk closer to the stream. Rhododendron grew thick on the hillsides, which should be beautiful in July, and in the spring the area has many colorful wildflowers. At 0.7 mile, we passed the intersection with Whitehouse Cliff Trail leading uphill to an overlook point, the side trail

to it rough to navigate for some, but with fine views. A half-mile further, the White Oak Flats Trail intersected. This trail, a more moderate one, travels along Long Branch stream to intersect with several interior park trails like the Hidden Lake Trail, the Birchfield Camp Trail, and the Headwaters Trail.

We continued alongside the stream on our hike into the Flint Creek Trail. Clear trail signs showed us the turns and intersections to the different park trails and corresponding colored markers on the trees helped to mark the trail routes as well. After crossing a few bridges, one a long log bridge across a stream, we came to the Flint Creek Battle Site. John Sevier led a raid here against the Chero-

kee 227 years ago during the Chickamauga Wars, leading his men into this remote area in two feet of snow on a January day in 1789. An open field marks the spot, without a sign, but a historical marker is planned for this site in future.

This lovely wilderness park offers an opportunity to take a walk or hike into a remote area with beautiful streams, fine overlooks, and natural beauties in a pristine undeveloped area.

MIDDLE TENNESSEE STATE PARK INDEX

MIDDLE TENNESSEE PARKS

Cumberland Mountain

Johnsonville

Montgomery Bell

Dunbar Cave

Edgar Evins State Park

Middle Tennessee - DeKalb County
Park Address: 1630 Edgar Evins Park Rd, Sliver Point, TN 38582
Park Size: 6,292 acres   Month Visited: April
Directions: From I-40 between Cookeville and Nashville, take
exit #268 at State Hwy 96/Valley Road. Drive four miles to park
entrance at the intersection of Hwy 141.

Park Description:

Maps show that Edgar Evins State Park sprawls across two peninsulas
jutting out into Center Hill Reservoir, so the first surprise on entering the area
is to find that the bulk of the park lies high above the lake on rolling hills and
rocky bluffs. The park roads wind through wooded forestland along the Eastern
Highland Rim with steep inclines dropping down to the lakeside throughout.
Many layered limestone cliffs and rocky outcroppings lie around the park, especially near the campground area. The woods in Edgar Evins State Park are
alive with owls, bald eagles, and songbirds, including some rare species like the
wood thrush, eastern wood pee-wee, and the cerulean warbler.

The park was built in the 1960s and 1970s and dedicated in 1975. It is
named for a State Senator and Smithville businessman James Edgar Evins who
played a role in the development of the Center Hill Dam and Reservoir. The
Evins family also helped to push for the establishment of a state park along the

lake's boundaries.

After passing the entrance sign, the road winds uphill through the woods and around a curve to arrive at a side road leading to the visitor center. The site spreads across a wooded hillside with a high observation tower rising above it. The stairs to the top of the tower begin inside the center and climb upward in a circular fashion to the observation plat-

form at the top. From the tower's summit, visitors can look out across the lake to the Center Hill Dam and—with binoculars—see many birds and other natural wildlife. Around the visitor center are rustic rock walls, flowerbeds, benches, picnic tables, and shady trees, making this a scenic spot. Beside the parking lot below the center, one of the first hiking trails in the park begins, the two mile Highland Rim Loop Trail. The trail drops steeply down through the woods to skirt along the edges of Center Hill Lake before climbing back uphill again to come out behind the visitor center. The trail is noted for its wildflowers, birds, and butterflies in spring, and inside the center visitors can pick up fliers with names of species one might see. Rangers also lead informative hikes on this and other trails to help visitors identify the diversity of birds, butterflies, and flowers in the park.

The next turn off the main road drops down to a scenic picnic area on the lake and the Edgar Evins Marina. Along the lakeside are three cov-

ered picnic pavilions with rock chimneys. Closer to the entrance sign for the marina is a lovely shaded picnic site on the hillside with a children's play park beside it. A sidewalk curls down from the picnic area to the marina which has 300 boat slips, a restaurant, and a gift shop—all open year round. Slips and pontoon boats can be rented at the marina, and the marina sells fishing supplies and gas. Fishing licenses can also be bought in the marina. With the Center Hill Reservoir sprawling over 18,000 acres, fishing is popular on the water and along the banks. Bass, walleye, trout, catfish, bluegill, and crappie are caught and the lake is host to several major fishing tournaments during the year.

Edgar Evins Park has approximately eleven miles of hiking trails. Continuing

• Visitor Center * Cabins * Swimming * Picnic Pavilions
* Playgrounds * Fishing * Camping - RV Sites * Hiking Trails
* Marina * Boat Rentals * Boat Launch Ramp * Interpretive Center
* Planned Programs * Gift Shop * Restaurant * Water Skiing

beyond the marina area, deeper into the park, leads to the pullover parking area for the start of two more hiking trails, the Millennium and Merritt Ridge trails. The Millennium Trail is a 2.5 miles loop walk. It descends to the lake and passes old rock walls and fences of 1940s home sites. The Merritt Ridge Trail is a five-mile extension of the Millennium Trail, climbing up a steep ridge before looping back to meet the Millennium Trail again. Taking both trails creates an 8 miles long round-trip hike, noted to be strenuous.

Beyond these trails the park road climbs once more before dropping off to the right to the campground area along Center Hill Lake. The Edgar Evins Campground here is an unusual one with most of the 60 campsites built as wooden platforms jutting off the roadsides, many with lake views. Each platform site has a picnic table and grill, can accommodate tents and motor homes up to 33 feet, with some platforms large enough for a 40-foot motor home. Around the campground area are three bathhouses, a dump station, a laundry facility, a fire circle, and a group of primitive campsites close to the lakeside. A meeting area that can be rented by the public is available in the campground building. It seats approximately 30 people with tables and chairs, has a restroom, and kitchenette. A one-mile Marina Trail links the campground area to the marina, and there are fine views to the marina from many spots in the campground.

Edgar Evins State Park has two paved boat ramps within the developed portion of the park and a third outside the park off Highway 70. A road beyond the campground winds steeply down to the main boat ramps. Boaters were lined up waiting to launch into the lake on the warm spring weekend we visited. A big picnic area sprawls between the boat ramps and the views across the lake are beautiful.

Beyond the boat ramp toward the end of the main park lies a small Interpretive Center. Inside the building are displays, historical photos of early settlers and the nearby area, interesting pictures showing the building of Center Hill Dam, nature artifacts, arrowheads, rocks, hornet and bird nests, and more. Across the street from the Interpretive Center is another of the park's hiking trails, the Evins Ridge Nature Trail. This half-mile pathway climbs up the ridge and around through the woods in a short loop.

A road behind the Interpretive Center leads to the lodge cabins in Edgar Evins Park. These accommodations look more like linked condos than rustic cabins. Each has a kitchen, bath, bedroom, and back porch with lake views. Behind the cabins, closer to the lake, is a nice swimming pool with broad steps

leading down into the shallow end of the pool. Beside the pool is a wide patio with a small boat dock nearby for guests.

Further down the main road at the far end of the park is a larger, public boat dock reaching out into the lake. This is a nice spot for views across the lake and a good place to spread out a blanket to have a quiet picnic.

History Note.

Archeological surveys of the Center Hill area, conducted by the Smithsonian Institution, located several mound sites and relics of prehistoric villages of Native Americans. Traces of early settlers can be found around many areas of the park. One spot is the Dunham Cemetery. Alexander Dunham, who died in 1878, was an early settler in the area. and he and other family members are buried on this quiet hillside. A short trail leads to the old cemetery, which has mostly rough rock markers. However, a clearer marker was later created and added to identify the burial site. The cemetery trail lies just past the Millennium and Merritt Ridge Trails parking area. Watch for an unmarked turn to the right. The path leads uphill to the cemetery and around to the

road again on what a ranger called an old deer path.

Sgt. Alvin C. York State Park

Middle Tennessee - Fentress County
Park Address: 2609 North York Hwy, Pall Mall, TN 38577
Park Size: 343 acres   Month Visited: May
Directions: From I-40 at Crossville, take Hwy 127 north to Pall Mall.

Park Description:

The Sgt. Alvin C. York State Park is a small, preserved historic site. The park is located in a scenic valley along a bend of the Wolf River. On the main park road, and the Wild River Loop around the property, can be found

York's house, an old mill, a general store, Sgt. York's burial ground, and other historic buildings and landmarks. Few soldiers of World War I have been more recognized than Alvin York for his distinguished service and bravery.

No clear entrance leads into the York State Park, but after passing a park sign and rounding a bend in the road, visitors will spot the York Country Store on the right. A row of rocking chairs sits on a rustic fromt porch and the store sells ice cream, snacks, and souvenirs. Not far from the country store, on the left, is the Alvin C. York & Sons General Merchandise building and visitors center. Inside, visitors can view a free film *Legacy In Action* about York's life, schedule a tour, and see historic artifacts.

Across the street from the visitor center is a World War I tank, a recreated 200-foot WW I trench, and the York family's large two-story Colonial-Revival-style homeplace. The first floor of the house is now a museum and free tours are available. A short 0.6 mile trail leads to a swinging bridge over the Wolf River and to a church and burial site on the loop road. Both sites can be seen readily by driving around the loop road. Just after the York home on the left is the Grist Mill and a shady park with a covered pavilion, playground, and picnic tables beside the banks of the Wolf River. Continuing around the loop road past the Grist Mill takes visitors by the York

Chapel, scenic farmlands, and the York Bible School before coming to the York Cemetery across the street from the Wolf River Methodist Church. In the cemetery is Alvin York's and other family members' grave sites.

History Note.

One of the most decorated and celebrated soldiers in American history, Sgt. Alvin York (1887-1964) at first applied for a conscientious objector status when drafted in 1917 but later changed his thoughts. While serving in the Army in France in World War I, York led a handful of men in a counterattack and capture of 132 German soldiers. He received many distinguished awards including the Medal of Honor from General Pershing.

After the war York returned to Tennessee, where in 1922 the Rotary Club of Nashville, in honor of his military contributions, gifted him with a 400-acre farm and two-story home in Pall Mall, where he and his wife Grace raised eight children. York opened a general store across from his home and later purchased a two-story gristmill on the banks of the Wolf River nearby.

In 1941 the movie based on his life *Sergeant York* was released and attained 11 Oscar nominations and the movie won two awards. The York farm and mill were added to the U.S. National Register of Historic Places in 1973 and in 1976 designated a National Historic Landmark.

Pickett CCC Memorial State Park

Middle Tennessee - Pickett County
Park Address: 4605 Pickett Park Hwy, Jamestown, TN 38556
Park Size: 865 acres   Month Visited: May
Directions: From I-40 to Exit 317 Crossville and then Hwy 127
north for 36 miles. Turn right on Hwy 154 and continue 12 miles
to park entrance.

Park Description:

　　　　Pickett State Park lies on the Tennessee-Kentucky border within the
19,200 acres of Picket State Forest and adjacent on the east to the Big South
Fork Recreation area. The park is an exceptionally beautiful one full of large
sandstone formations, high rocky bluffs, and other unusual geological treasures.
Within the grounds are picnic and camping areas, rental cabins, a swimming
area on a 12-acre lake, and an abundance of hiking trails. Pickett is a true paradise for hiking enthusiasts with the South Fork area also nearby.

　　　　One distinction of this park is its status as a Silver-Tier International
Dark Sky Park. On clear nights visibility into the night sky is exceptional.
From the Pickett-Pogue Astronomy Field visitors can observe a sky filled with
constellations, meteors, and The Milky Way. Pickett was the first state park in
the southeast to be listed as a certified dark sky viewing location, and the park
offers dark sky viewing events throughout the year at the Pogue Creek Canyon
State Natural Area off Highway 154 near the entrance.

A nice visitor center sits on the left of the highway leading into the main section of the park. In the center, visitors can attain a brochure, a hiking trail map, and other information. By request rangers can let visitors into the historic stone Civilian Conservation Corps (CCC) Museum that sits beside the center. The museum contains artifacts and photos from the

1930s era and an interactive touch-screen display in which actual CCC workers share their early memories of working in the park.

The road to the left beside the visitor center leads to picturesque Arch Lake. Alongside the 12 acres lake is a sand beach, a roped off swimming area, and a boathouse offering canoe and kayak rentals. Although the lake is small, fishing is permitted along the banks and a license can be attained at the park office. On a hillside above the swim area is a recreation lodge built by CCC workers, a shady playground, and picnic area. Nearby are an amphitheater, tennis courts, and a pavilion as well as access to several of the park's trails. Below the lodge visitors will quickly spot a long, inviting swinging bridge that leads across the lake to a second picnic pavilion on a rocky bluff.

Pickett State Park's main campground and some of the rental cabins can be found by taking the road to the right behind the visitor center. There are 20 rental cabins in the park. Five are rustic cabins of native stone, built by the CCC, the other 15 more modern ones. The campground offers 32 campsites with water and electric hookups, grills, and picnic tables. The campground has a children's play area, bathhouse, and dump station. There is also a nature center in the campground, a public picnic area, and access to more of the park's trails. On a high

Pickett State Park:
• Visitor Center * Cabins * Swimming * Picnic Pavilions * CCC Museum
* Playgrounds * Fishing * Camping * Hiking Trails * Boathouse
* Gift Shop * Tennis Courts * Stables * Canoe & Kayak Rentals

point in the campground is a scenic water tower, built by the CCC in the 1930s. Constructed over a well, this was the main water source for the park for many years and is still a back-up source of water when needed.

More than 58 miles of hiking trails wander through Pickett State Park and the surrounding forest. The park brochure lists 14 different trails, although many intersect and interlink. Two trails lie across from each other on Highway 154 entering the park— Indian Rock House Trail and Hazard Cave Trail. On the right side of the road, Indian Rock House Trail leads down to a stunning rocky sandstone bluff. The path to the bluff is only 700 feet in length, an easy walk for anyone to take. At the trail's end, sandstone bluffs tower high overhead with a narrow passage wandering below them, like walking through a cave. The rare and endangered sandwort plant grows in the loose sand of the rockhouse and in July has tiny white flowers on its stems.

Across the highway the Hazard Cave Trail weaves a quarter of a mile to another large rock house structure. This trail is a steep downhill climb winding down several tiers of rock stairways, making this a difficult trail for any with knee, hip or health problems. A cave-like sweep of pocked rocky sandstone bluffs lies at the bottom of the trail with a wooden walkway following along below the bluffs. This is a spectacular rock structure to view, and at night from May to September glow-worms can be seen on the rock walls. Like fireflies, glow-worms shine in the dark, giving off a pale blue light. The glow-worms are actually larvae that later become gnats (*orphelia fultani*). These larvae can be found in more abundance here than in any other place in the United States. The park naturalist offers night tours in summer to see the glow-worms at Hazard Cave.

In the interior of the Pickett State Park are many other nice hiking trails. We hiked to see the natural rock bridge on the 1.0 mile Natural Bridge Trail that begins near the Recreation Lodge, explored the 0.75 mile Lake View Trail, and walked part of the 3.0 miles Ridge Trail at the end of the loop road past the Recreation Lodge. Behind the campground area the Ladder Trail curls its way in a 1.0 mile loop to Thompson Creek and back, and at the end of the campground area is an interesting trail called the Island Trail. It winds across rocky bluffs, with the trail actually traveling on rock in many spots, to look down on the lake and across an old spillway dam between Arch Lake and the creek below. A piece of this trail, found behind the cabin suites on the hillside, drops down to a rock bridge arching over the water that Arch Lake is named for.

One of the most well-known and popular trails at Pickett State Park is the Hidden Passage Trail. To reach this trailhead, travel down Highway 154 past the visitor center and watch for the trail sign and parking area on the right. The trail wanders in a 10 miles long loop toward the border of South Fork Recreation Area and back, but a shorter 0.6 mile walk will lead to the Hidden Passage area the trail is named for. Here a narrow, almost hidden, opening leads through a rocky bluff, with benches and lookout areas around the sandstone area for enjoying the unusual geological formations. For a longer hike, another mile beyond the Hidden Passage will lead to Crystal Falls, a cascade spill over rock shelves with a picturesque pool below.

History Note:

Pickett State Park was developed by the Civilian Conservation Corps (CCC) after the Stearns Coal and Lumber Company donated the park's land in 1933 to the State of Tennessee. The CCC crews built the original ranger station, lodge, and early cabins—using locally quarried sandstone— and they created the park's lake and hiking trails. The original structures, many with beautiful gabled roofs and impressive stone fireplaces, are now on the National Register of Historic Places. In 2012 the park dedicated a life-sized CCC statue to the workers instrumental in the development of the park and placed it beside the CCC museum. The commemorative statue is the first of its kind in Tennessee.

Cumberland Mtn State Park

Middle Tennessee - Cumberland County
Park Address: 24 Office Drive, Crossville, TN 38555
Park Size: 1,720 acres   Month Visited: June
Directions: From I-40 East from Nashville to Exit 317. South on
US Hwy 127 for nine miles. The park entrance is on the right.
From Knoxville, I-40W to Exit 322. Left at exit to Hwy 127 to
park at 6 miles.

Park Description:

Cumberland Mountain State Park lies on a section of the Cumberland
Plateau, an upland region extending from Alabama to New York. The park's
1,720 acre tract was acquired by the government in 1938 to provide a recreational
area for the homestead families brought to the area through Roosevelt's New Deal
program. By building a dam on Byrd Creek, Byrd Lake was created, which is
now the centerpiece for the park.

A visitor center lies a short distance down the road from the main entrance. In the center visitors can pick up brochures and a map of the park. A
detailed map of the campground area and an easy to follow trail guide can be
found on one of the park's fliers, and a topographical trail map is also available.
Cumberland Mountain has six hiking trails, all marked with colored blazes, since
some paths interlink. Most are short, easy to moderate walks, with none over
eight miles in length.

The Byrd Creek Trail starts directly across from the visitor center. The

2.55 miles loop pathway winds along the shady banks of Byrd Creek, to cross it at two points, before wandering back to the trail's beginning. Other than the need to navigate a lot of rocks and exposed roots along the creekside, this is a nice walk to take and enjoy—even on a hot summer's day. A highlight on the trail is the rustic bridge built by a group of Eagle Scouts for a special project. If a lengthy

hike is desired, the beginning of the area's longest trail, the Overnight Trail, intersects this trail to wind for eight miles up the mountain to an overnight campsite and back again.

The road to Cumberland Mountain's fine campground area lies on the right just before the visitor center, leading to 140 campsites for tents and RVs. This is a popular campground, well-laid out with electrical services, bathhouses, a dump station, and all amenities including a camp store. A second road across from the campground area winds around to Cumberland Mountain Park's recreation building and swimming pool. The large Olympic-sized pool, with a diving area and separate children's wading pool, sits on a scenic site with a bathhouse and a snack bar. On the sunny June day we visited, the pool was full of visitors enjoying the day.

Beyond the visitor center, the main road winds across the Stone Arch Bridge and dam. This is one of the most scenic and photographed spots in the park. Built by the Civilian Conservation Corps (CCC), it is the largest masonry structure ever built by the Corps, 319 feet long with seven arches. An old mill

house, now called Mill House Lodge, lies down a side street before the bridge crossing. Originally a gristmill, it was designed by Quakers.

Across the bridge on the right is the beginning of another hiking trail, the Cumberland Plateau Trail, a one-mile loop walk. On the hill above the lake is a rustic lodge and the popular Homestead Harvest Restaurant. The restaurant

Cumberland Mountain State Park:

• Visitor Center * Cabins * Swimming * Picnic Pavilions * Museum
* Playgrounds * Fishing * Camping * Hiking Trails * Boathouse
* Gift Shop * Tennis Courts * Amphitheater * Canoe & Kayak Rentals

with its large picture windows, looks out over the lake and a broad patio full of tables and chairs. The Harvest Restaurant serves daily buffets, popular with visitors, and has a gift shop and three banquet meeting rooms downstairs that can be rented for private events. Along the lake is another of the park's walking trails, the Lake Trail, a broad easy trail following along the side of Byrd Lake for less than a mile. Fishing is allowed in the 35 acres lake along the banks, and ducks and geese enjoy the area along with the many visitors. An outdoor amphitheater sits on a rise by the lake's edge, a favorite spot for outdoor park activities and private events like the wedding we saw in progress the day we visited.

Beyond the restaurant, the park road twines around by picnic pavilions and a picnic area to climb a hill to a large playground with a volleyball court, ball field, tennis courts, more picnic tables, and the park's largest pavilion, popular for party rentals. Below the side road to the playground, the road continues to the cabin rental area and to a boat dock on the lake. Visitors can rent kayaks, paddleboats, canoes, and small fishing boats from May through October. Spanning across the lake is a wooden bridge, a part of the Pioneer Short Loop Trail, which travels for two miles around the edge of Byrd Lake and back again. There are scenic views of the lake along the way and at the other end of the trail the pathway crosses over a swinging bridge. A second section of the Pioneer Trail can extend the hike for three more miles if desired, rising into the woods and back.

An added feature of the Cumberland Mountain State Park is the Jack

Nicklaus Bear Trace Golf Course, opened in 1998. It can be found by leaving the main section of the park and driving south on Hwy 127 to the golf course entrance sign on the right. A short side road, Wild Plum Lane, leads to the golf course and a nice clubhouse. The eighteen-hole golf course is ranked as one of the top ten golf courses in Tennessee and utilizes many natural features in the 6,900-yard, par-72 layout course. The course features a driving range and has yearly memberships and senior rates available.

Cumberland Mountain State Park's many amenities, and its location near other popular sites in and around Crossville, Tennessee, make this a favorite and loved destination. Park rangers conduct many events of interest, especially in the summer, and the Fourth of July parade is particularly popular—in which visitors avidly participate. Put this park on your "to visit" list.

History Note.

A mile before the park entance at the intersection of Hwy 127 and Hwy 68, is the Homestead Tower and Museum. Although just outside the park boundary, this site is linked to the history of the park and surrounding area. The Homesteads was one of the more successful of Franklin D. Roosevelt's relocation settlements as a part of the New Deal in the 1930s. Approximately 250 struggling families were relocated and settled to the area, which included over 10,000 acres.

Homestead buildings and houses were constructed of hand-quarried Crab Orchard and fieldstone and many still remain, including over a dozen structures within the state park built by Civilian Conservation Corps workers. The Homesteads Tower Museum, once the administrative offices for the settlement,

contains old photos and artifacts from Homesteader families and a film that tells the history of the settlement's development. The high tower is a water tank that can house 50,000 gallons of water. In 1988 the U.S. Government placed the tower, adjacent school house, and remaining 218 homes on the National Register of Historic Places.

Cordell Hull Birthplace State Park

Middle Tennessee - Pickett County
Park Address: 1300 Cordell Hull Memorial Drive, Byrdstown TN 38549
Park Size: 58 acres   Month Visited: June
Directions: From I-40 at Cookeville, take Hwy 111 north to Livingston to Byrdstown. Turn left on Hwy 325 at Byrdstown which leads directly to the park.

Park Description:

Due to the efforts of supporters and financing from the State of Tennessee, the Cordell Hull State Park was opened in 1997 on 58 acres in Pickett County to pay tribute to the life of Legislator Cordell Hull. The park property includes a log cabin replica, created like the early home Cordell Hull was born in, the Cordell Hull Museum and visitor center, and a park office and meeting facility.

Inside the visitor center and Cordell Hull Museum are informational pieces about the park and the legislator's life, as well as paintings, papers, photographs, and artifacts. The Hull Library and Archives room holds the more valuable documents, books, and items preserved from Hull's lifetime.   A walkway leads beyond the museum to the park office and meeting facility and on to the Hull cabin with a fenced garden spot below it. The cabin is fully furnished with period pieces and memorabilia. In each room, visitors can push a wall button to

hear an interesting discussion about the room and its contents.

Across the street from the historical site is a parking area for the 2.5 miles Bunkum Cave Loop Trail. The shaded woods trail is well maintained and an easy to moderate walk for all ages. Along its route are many wooden bridges and benches, and in the spring wildflowers can be spotted in abundance along the way. Near the cave entrance are two wooden overlooks built to help visitors enjoy looking down over the cave opening and to the rocky ledges across from it. Steep steps lead down to the cave, 30 feet tall and 100 feet wide. Deep inside the cave are stalactites, stalagmites, and layers of white gypsum crystal but a cave permit from the park office is required to explore the cave past the entrance area.

History Note.

Cordell Hull (1871-1955) was an American politician, born in a log cabin in Pickett County, Tennessee. After studying law and entering politics at an early age, he was elected to the Tennessee House of Representatives, before resigning to serve as a captain in the Tennessee Volunteer Infantry in the Spanish-American War. After the war, Hull returned to the legal profession before being elected again to the

House of Representatives and later to the Senate. He became Secretary of State under Franklin D. Roosevelt for 11 years, the longest term for a Secretary of State in U.S. history. In his distinguished 30-year political career, he helped to author the Federal Income Tax Bill, the Inheritance Tax Law and worked tirelessly to create the United Nations for which he was awarded the Nobel Peace Prize.

Standing Stone State Park

Middle Tennessee - Overton County
Park Address: 1674 Standing Stone Park Hwy, Hilham, TN 38568
Park Size: 1,042 acres   Month Visited: June
Directions: Take Exit 288 I-40 (Livingston/Sparta exit). Take
Hwy 111 N to Livingston, turn left on Hwy 52 West (toward Ce-
lina) to the park entrance.

Park Description:

Standing Stone State Park lies nestled in the middle of the 11,000 acres Standing Stone State Forest. The 1,042 acres park was created in the 1930s as a recreational facility for families relocated to the area as a part of Franklin D. Roosevelt's New Deal projects. Evidence of the Civilian Conservation Corps' handiwork can be seen in many of the park structures and buildings and in the dam built to create 69 acres Kelly Lake that spreads in a four-fingered X-shape in the middle of the property. Along the sides of the lake and above it on the high ridges are the park's main recreational areas—a campground with 36 tent and trailer sites, picnic areas, playgrounds, tennis courts, volleyball and basketball courts, an Olympic-sized swimming pool, bathhouse, and snack bar.

The visitor center has a gift shop and nature display with a nearby amphitheater for outdoor programs. In September, the national Rolley Hole Marble Championship and Festival is always held at the park. Across the street from the center is a rustic meeting facility, called The Tea Room, with indoor and outdoor

areas for conferences and group events. Latticed down shady side roads branching out beside the Tea Room and the visitor center are the park's rental cabins. There are 21 cabins, most with cute porches for enjoying the out-of-doors.

At the end of the cabin road behind the visitor center is an access point to the park's eight mile Lake Trail hiking loop, labeled as the Cabin Spur on the park's hiking map. The hiking loop winds its way around Kelly Lake, climbing the ridges above it or looping down to walk along the lakeside. There are several places to access the trail around the park, so visitors can hike only pieces of the trail as desired. One access point to the Lake Trail can be found by walking across a swinging bridge at the dam. Beside the dam are more recreational areas and a boat rental

facility. Following the road across the dam leads around to the old Fisk House on the park's property, named for an early settler, with another access point to the Lake Trail beside it. For more explorations, visitors can drive around to Beach Road on the back of the park, a popular spot for fishing on the lake's banks.

History Note.

Standing Stone State Park is named for a historic 16-foot monolith that once stood nearby on the Cumberland Plateau. According to legend, the giant stone was once revered by the Native Americans of the area and marked the boundary between Shawnee and Cherokee land. It served as a guidepost for hunting parties and early settlers, but the stone was unfortunately dynamited in 1893

to make way for railroad construction. In 1895, a preservationist group created a monument to the memory of the standing stone with a preserved piece of the stone at the top of it. You can see it in front of the Monterey Public Library in nearby Monterey, Tennessee.

Cummins Falls State Park

Middle Tennessee - Jackson County
Park Address: 390 Cummins Falls Lane, Cookeville, TN 38501
Park Size: 211 acres   Month Visited: June
Directions: From I-40 near Cookeville, take Exit 280 onto TN-56 north for 7.7 miles. Turn right on Hwy 190, then left on Cummins Mill Rd for 2.9 miles, then left onto Blackburn Ford Rd for 0.2 miles to park entrance.

Park Description:

Cummins Falls State Park became Tennessee's 54th state park in 2011. The park's major attraction is its spectacular waterfall and swimming hole, named one of the ten best swimming holes in the U.S. by *Travel + Leisure* magazine. Even on a weekday, the park's large gravel parking lot was packed with cars—most spending the day swimming and enjoying the falls.

As a newer park, Cummins has few amenities at this point and no formal visitor center, but there is a restroom at the end of the parking lot and an informational kiosk. From behind the kiosk a dirt and gravel trail leads to a sign reading "Trail Head" that marks the entrance to the path leading to the falls and back in a 2.5 miles loop. A short distance down the trail the path forks, with a sign directing visitors to the right to continue on the Downstream Trail to the bottom of the falls or to the left to the Waterfall Overlook.

The trail to the base of the falls is not an improved trail and it leads downhill on a route that is rocky and steep in spots. Park signs warn the trail is potentially dangerous. When the trail arrives at the Blackburn Fork State Scenic River, the ongoing route wanders in and out of the river, knee deep or waist deep depending on the river's depth, for a quarter of a mile before arriving at the base of the falls. The trail is by no means easy, even for those who come prepared to wade the river, but for many it is worth the challenge to spend a day at the falls.

For the less adventurous and for most visitors not planning an afternoon in the water, it is only a 0.4 mile walk to a fine overlook with spectacular views down into the gorge to the waterfall. Cummins Falls, the eighth largest waterfall in volume in Tennessee, drops 75 feet in a large curtain of water over a rocky bluff to a stair-step ledge and then into a deep, wide plunge pool. On the hot June day we visited, swimmers were gathered in droves around the falls—sitting on the rocky ledges with their feet in the cascades, enjoying a shower under the falling curtain of water, or swimming in the deep pool below.

For a picnic at the park, there are tables across from the parking lot in a wooded area behind a colorful quilt sign. Behind the picnic area are the remains of the old Cummins home. The park property first belonged to a Revolutionary War soldier, Sergeant Blackburn, who was given the land as a pension in the 1790s. Then in 1825, John Cummins bought the property, farmed it

and built several mills on it. The land stayed in the Cummins family for more than 180 years, the falls only well-known and enjoyed by locals, until a combined public-private effort made it possible for the state to purchase the property for a park.

Burgess Falls State Park

Middle Tennessee - White County
Park Address: 4000 Burgess Falls Drive, Sparta, TN 38583
Park Size: 350 acres   Month Visited: June
Directions: From I-40 near Cookeville, exit on Hwy 135 south to park entrance.

Park Description:

The Burgess Falls State Natural Area lies along The Falling Water River in White County. The park is named after Tom Burgess, a Revolutionary War

veteran who settled the area in the 1790s and built a gristmill and later a sawmill on the river. In 1973 the area was dedicated as a state natural area. The park is known primarily for its waterfalls but also has a fishing pier, playground, pavilion, picnic area, outdoor amphitheater, and a small park office. Adjacent to the office be-

side the upper parking area is the Native Butterfly Garden. Several trails weave through the garden with benches, an arched bridge, and an abundance of wildflowers chosen to attract butterflies. Beside the garden, a wooden walkway leads down to a fishing pier that overlooks the river and the old Burgess Falls Dam. We had lunch on a picnic table on this pier before exploring the park.

The lower parking lot at Burgess lies beside a large picnic pavilion with restrooms where events can be held. A playground and picnic tables are also scattered nearby. Behind the pavilion, a path leads down to the river and to the 1.5 miles River Trail, an out-and-back trail that leads along the river to four waterfalls.

The Burgess Falls Dam diverted Falling Water River so that it created a long gorge below the dam, dropping in levels to eventually meet Center Hill Lake downstream—and creating several beautiful waterfalls along its way. The first falls, Falling Water Cascades, is a 10 foot series of cascades spilling over rocky ledges in the river. Many people fish or picnic on the bank near the cascades. Beyond the pretty mossy cascades a park trail sign shows the distance to the next three waterfalls. One hundred feet beyond the sign the river drops 30 feet again over a rock shelf to form First Falls. A wooden observation deck is built along the trail where visitors can look out over the falls. Beyond the overlook, the trail winds on along the river, often working its way over rocks, alongside boulders, or

over ridges on stairs built along the riverbank. At one-half mile from the trail sign Falling River drops 80 feet to form Middle Falls, a wide spill of water tumbling over a rocky bluff. A large wood overlook allows visitors a nice vantage point for enjoying views of the falls.

After the trail climbs up and around another ridge, the final falls and overlook is reached. Big Falls, or Burgess Falls, spills over a high rocky bluff to drop for 136 feet down into a pool at the bottom. It's an incredible sight. The rocky ledge walls around the pool rise 100-200 feet high. The falls is noted as one of the most impressive in Tennessee, and even though the trail to the falls takes a little care to navigate, the views of Burgess Falls and the canyon below it make the walk well worthwhile.

On the return hike, a one-mile side trail can be taken on Ridgetop Trail with views down to the river and canyon. An alternate return route, if preferred, follows the gravel Service Road. This route is a little easier underfoot than the path along the river—but you miss seeing the waterfalls again by walking it. The beauty of the falls at this park make it a site many return to for more than one visit.

Fall Creek Falls State Park

Middle Tennessee - Van Buren & Bledsoe Counties
Park Address: 10821 Park Road, Spencer, TN 38585
Park Size: 26,000 acres   Month Visited: June
Directions: From I-40 from Nashville or Knoxville to Exit 317
Crossville. Follow US Hwy 127 south to Hwy 30 at Pikeville.
Turn right on #30 and follow to park entrance.

Park Description:

Fall Creek Falls State Park is centered on the upper Cane Creek Gorge, a vast region that stretches for 15 miles from the Cane Creek Cascades in the middle of the park to the mouth of Caney Fork River. The old Liberty Hill School, near the park's north entrance, serves as a reminder of the hardy settlers who once farmed and logged on this rugged plateau. As Cane Creek River moves through the gorge, it drops several hundred feet at different junctures along its route, creating a series of stunning waterfalls. There are six waterfalls in the 26,000 acres park and the park is named for the highest of these, Fall Creek Falls, which spills over a rocky ledge into a deep pool below. It is often thought of as the centerpiece of the area.

The first falls in this large and well-visited state park can be found after entering the north end of the park behind the Nature Center and visitor area. Inside the center are interpretive displays, a gift shop, and an indoor theater. Be sure to pick up park maps, brochures, and a hiking guide while there. Behind the Nature Center, a winding trail leads to a long series of wooden steps, dropping to a wide pool at the base of Cane Creek Cascades. On hot summer days, many visitors play in the cool water or sit in the sun on the broad rocks. Behind the Cascades a long, bouncy suspension bridge leads across the river to two hiking trails. The easy Woodland Trail weaves left toward the campground area. The Gorge Overlook Trail winds to the right in a one-mile loop passing several overlooks that offer views to the falls and gorge below, including one at Fall Creek Falls.

Beyond the cascades area, Cane Creek River curls around a bend to drop over a wide rocky bluff, forming 85 foot long Cane Creek Falls. Nearby Rockhouse Creek also spills over this high bluff to form a second 125 foot narrow waterfall called Rockhouse Falls. A trail in front of the Nature Center leads to a lookout with views to both falls and the gorge be-

low—an impressive sight. Although Cane Creek Falls is noted to have the largest volume of water of all the park's falls, on most summer days—like when we visited—the falls often appear as little more than a trickle and Rockhouse Falls may not be visible at all. For a closer look at Cane Creek and Rockhouse Falls, a rough, steep hiking trail, called the Cable Trail, leads down to the pool below the bluffs.

Across the street from the Nature Center are restrooms, pavilions, a picnic area, and a park. On down the street are the camping areas. The park has 222 campsites in five areas, with sites suitable for tent and RV camping, and six bathhouses. Near the campground area is the Village Green Complex including the Fall Creek Falls Outfitters and General Store, a snack bar, and a coin laundry. Nearby are an outdoor amphitheater, a zipline adventure park, a ballfield, tennis and basketball courts, picnic pavilions, and an Olympic-sized pool, situated on a beautiful spot by the lake. We stopped for ice cream at the poolside snack bar and enjoyed watching kids dive into the swimming pool below.

After leaving the complex and camping areas, the park road crosses the dam over 45-acre Fall Creek Lake to weave through the forest to the rental cabins and boat dock. Canoes, kayaks, paddleboats, and aluminum fishing boats can be rented at the dock and fishing is available on the lake and creeks throughout the park. There are

Fall Creek Falls State Park:

• Nature Center * Cabins * Swimming Pool * Picnic Pavilions * Golf
* Playgrounds * Fishing * Camping * Hiking Trails * Horse Stables
* Snack Shop * Tennis Courts * Amphitheater * Canoe & Kayak Rentals

30 rental cabins in two scenic sections near the dock. The Landside Cabins are located on a wooded hill overlooking the lake while the Fisherman Cabins are situated right beside Fall Creek Lake, many jutting out over the water.

A short distance beyond the cabins is the lovely Fall Creek Falls Inn and Conference Center. The large inn has meeting rooms for events and conferences, a full restaurant, and 145 guest rooms with balconies looking out over the lake. Gaul's Galley Restaurant has daily southern-style buffets and offers a fine dining experience. The inn has its own private swimming pool and game room and guests can enjoy walking the 1.35 miles paved trail from the inn along the lake to the dam, a shaded, easy walking trail for all ages and abilities.

A nearby side road leads to one of the group camps. The park has two group camp facilities with cabins and bathhouses and a fully equipped group lodge. Biking is popular at Fall Creek Falls and visitors can enjoy 24 miles of backwoods trails or simply ride bikes throughout the park. Also for outdoor enthusiasts, there are 35 miles of hiking trails. Some of the park's hiking trails are easily accessible with well-marked signs while others lie in more remote areas or wind off of other trails, not as easy to locate. The park provides a hiking guide map but not all the trails are shown on it, as the park is so large. We walked the popular trails to the waterfalls, explored parts of the Paw Paw Trail, the Woodland and Campground trails, and walked the lake trail near the inn. We also hiked a portion of the Copperhead Rock Climbers Trail and a section of the Overnight Trail. Many of the park trails are very rocky and difficult to navigate while others are

only moderate in difficulty. To cool off, a dip in the George Hole on Cane Creek is always fun.

Near the inn and cabins, a side road leads to the Fall Creek Falls Overlook. A short path leads from the parking lot to the overlook with its panoramic views. Fall Creek Falls cascades over the top of the cliff side to drop dramatically for 256 feet into a plunge pool below. In summer the water volume in the falls is limited but in spring and fall, especially after heavy rains, the rush of water over the rocks can be an impressive sight. In wet seasons a twin waterfall, Coon Creek Falls, can also be seen spilling 250 feet over the cliff nearby, but in summer this falls is rarely visible. Near the overlook, a steep 0.4 mile trail winds down to the base of the falls, advised to be a difficult hike.

The road beyond the overlook winds into the one-way Gorge Scenic Drive Motor Nature Trail, a delightful one-way road along the edge of the gorge with many roadside pullovers leading to stunning views. At several points overlooks have been built with informational signs, like Caplenor Point and Millikan's Overlook. Also, a side road off the nature trail leads to the parking area for Piney Creek Falls. A short rocky trail leads downhill to an overlook to the falls, a long narrow plume spewing over a bluff. Another trail from the parking lot leads to a high suspension bridge over Piney Falls Creek.

Two additional assets to the park are an 18-hole golf course and a riding stable. The golf course, designed by Joe Lee, has a driving range, practice tee, and snack bar while the riding stable offers a four-miles guided horseback ride through the forest. This is truly a state park that has something for everyone.

Rock Island State Park

Middle Tennessee - Warren & White Counties
Park Address: 82 Beach Road, Rock Island, TN 38581
Park Size: 883 acres   Month Visited: July
Directions: From I-40 from Nashville or Knoxville to Exit 288 at
Cookeville. Follow US Hwy 111 South, merging left on Hwy 70
and then turn right on Hwy 136. In the town of Rock Island, turn
left under the arch onto Hwy 287 and follow into the park.

Park Description:

  The main acreage of Rock Island State Park lies in Warren County in a
peninsula of land between Caney Fork River and Collins River, with an additional
section across the Caney Fork River in White County. The park, created in 1969,
is known for its scenic waterfalls, bluffs, hiking trails, and sand beach.
  The earliest settlers to the Rock Island community arrived in the later
1790s. The area was on the Old Kentucky Road and many travelers often passed
through. A tavern and a ferry developed and around the time of the Civil War, a
mill was built to harness the Caney Fork's power. The first mill was washed out
completely by floods but a second, the Great Falls Cotton Mill, was built after
the Civil War and operated from 1892 until 1902. The old mill building still sits
by the Caney Fork River just inside the park boundary. It is now on the National
Register of Historic Places. After crossing the Collins River and entering the
park, the mill is the first major site you will see. Across the street from the mill
is the Spring Castle, a picturesque stone springhouse, used by mill workers for

refrigeration purposes.

At the parking lot beside the old mill is the Great Falls Overlook. From the big wooden overlook, visitors can look down over stunning Great Falls, a 30 foot horseshoe waterfall cascading over the edges of a rocky bowl. This point has several beautiful sections of falls and cascades, all visible from the overlook area.

Continuing down the road from the overlook, leads to the Old Mill picnic area, pavilion, and restrooms. At the end of the road a sign points the way down to the Old Mill Trail. Another overlook lies a short distance down the trail, giving stunning views out over the Caney Fork River Gorge. The ongoing 0.5 mile trail to the base of the gorge is very steep, with many wood and rock stair steps, often muddy and slick, winding down the ridge side to a swimming hole below.

Back on the main road, on the left side of the roadway, is the parking area for the Collins River Trail. Rock Island Park has nine hiking trails, each distinct and different, and the Collins River Trail is the longest, a three miles loop that circles around the outer edge of the Collins River peninsula. The trail is a cool, shady woods walk, following a ridgeline above the river. Occasionally there are views down to the river below. A new connector trail leads over to cemeteries of early settlers to extend the hike. A sign says the Collins River Trail is for both hiking and biking, but mountain bikes would be needed.

The visitor center can be found in the second section of the park by turning right onto Beach Road at the main entrance sign. At the center are informational brochures, hiking trail maps, and more. Past the visitor center are side roads to tent campsites and two picnic areas. At the back of the Blue Hole Picnic Area are two more hiking trails. The Eagle Trail starts across a short wooden bridge and weaves its way through the woods for 0.7 mile to connect to the picnic area at Badger Flats. The trail has some ups-and-downs, roots and rocks to navigate, but is basically a moderate walk. The short but steep 0.5 mile Blue Hole

Trail also begins near the Eagle Trail, starting its way down a long span of wooden stairs to lead to an overlook, and then on down another steep span of metal steps to the gorge below. Views of the Blue Hole pool are visible from several points along the way. This is a spawning spot for walleye fish that will later find their

way into Center Hill Lake and a popular fishing spot. At the base of the trail, a lovely series of cascading waterfalls spill over a rock wall, making a pretty sight. Be sure you wear boots or strong shoes on all park trails.

Beyond the picnic areas, a turn to the left winds back to the main campground area of the park, and to tennis courts, a playground, and the colorful rental cabins. Rock Island Park's rental cabins are some of the nicest we've seen in the state parks and look like small suburban homes. All have three bedrooms, two baths, and are nicely furnished. The campground has sites suitable for 50 RVs and trailers, and it has two bathhouses, a dump station, a big picnic pavilion, nice playground, volleyball court, and a Nature Center. Many flowers and plants are identified by

markers around the center. Near the entrance to the campground area is the beginning of the short 0.5 mile Moonshine Trail, leading down to a site where an old still used to sit. Across from the campground are tennis courts and behind the courts, the 1.7 miles Bluff Trail begins. The early part of this trail also leads to the park's rustic amphitheater built by a group of Eagle Scouts.

Returning to the main park road leads to the Badger Flat Picnic area and the riverfront area of the park known as the Sandbar or "The Beach." A boat launch ramp and a wide sandy beach lie along the banks of the Caney Fork River, creating a popular spot for water play. There are fine views across the river to high rocky bluffs and down the river

toward the Center Hill Reservoir. The area

has ample parking, a bathhouse. and a large covered picnic pavilion looking out on the river.

The Twin Falls section of Rock Island State Park, on the other side of the Caney Fork River, was previously accessed by crossing over Great Falls Dam, but the road across the dam is now closed to traffic. The visitor center can provide clear directions to the Twin Falls area, which can be accessed now by following Hwy 287 from the park, turning left on Hwy 136, crossing the bridge, turning left on Power House Road at the park signs, and following until the road dead ends at the river and powerhouse. From the parking area, a steep set of stairs leads down to the Twin Falls Down River Trail. This is a beautiful 1.6 miles moderate hiking trail along the ridges above the Caney Fork River with spectacular views of the Twin Falls and its many cascades all along the way.

Twin Falls pours out from the walls of the gorge instead of over the gorge, dropping 80 feet into the river below. These glorious falls and cascades did not exist before 1925 when the Great Falls Dam was built. The damming of the water caused the river upstream to divert into underground limestone caverns, to then later pour out of the gorge walls below the powerhouse. Just above the powerhouse area two other trails wind down into the gorge to border the river. The 1.6 miles Downstream Trail is the more moderate one, with several small falls along the way, and the short 0.5 mile Upstream Trail the more strenuous. Kayakers love playing in the pools below the falls, but care is needed throughout this area and swimming is prohibited. Currents are swift and water is often released into the river from the powerhouse. Warning signs at many points caution swimmers and hikers to watch for sudden rises in water levels or to get out of the water should they hear siren warnings.

South Cumberland State Park

Middle Tennessee-Grundy, Franklin, Marion, Sequatchie Counties
Park Address: 11745 US Hwy 41, Monteagle, TN 37356
Park Size: 25,539 acres - spread out   Month Visited: July
Directions: To the main visitor center, from Chattanooga take I-24
north to Monteagle exit #135. Right on Hwy 41S for 4.5 miles,
following park signs to visitor center on left.

Park Description:

South Cumberland State Park is not a traditional state park confined to one main acreage area. Instead it is spread out in multiple sections and natural areas over a four-county area, with some of the park sections thirty minutes to an hour apart. To visit South Cumberland in a one-day trip means a person can only hit the highlights of the park's main areas. The place to begin an exploration journey of this area is at the main visitor center between Monteagle and Tracy City.

The visitor center has a wide variety of maps to help tourists locate the different sights, regions, and hiking trails within the park. The center and its acreage, once a golf course, opened as the hub for the South Cumberland Park in 1973. Around the center are picnic tables and a pavilion, where we ate our lunch, enjoying the barn swallows flying nearby. Next to the picnic area are tennis, volleyball, and basketball courts, horseshoes, a baseball field, and a playground. The 1.3 miles Meadow Trail winds its way through what was originally the old golf course. It's an easy walk through wildflower fields and alongside a pond.

Not far from the center is the Grundy Forest State Natural Area and the Fiery Gizzard Trail, which begins at a park area with a picnic pavilion and restrooms. The full 13 miles Fiery Gizzard Trail extends all the way to the southern Foster Falls area of the park. It is a strenuous and difficult hike, but popular with backcountry hiking enthusiasts. The average hiker might better enjoy the early part of the trail on what is known as the Grundy Forest Day Loop, a two-miles roundtrip hike that gives a taste of what the longer trail is like. It scrambles down rocky stairs and through the woods under giant trees, passing interesting geologic formations and under vast boulders. The trail then winds alongside cascading streams to the 9-foot Blue Hole waterfall and pool.

Southwest from the visitor center near Sewanee are the Carter State and Hawkins Cove Natural Areas and the Sewanee Natural Bridge. A short trail and a steep flight of stairs lead from the parking area to the bridge, a natural sandstone structure 25-feet high and 50-feet long. Visitors can walk across the bridge, peeping down into the sinkhole below. Nearby Buggytop Trail leads 2.2 miles to Lost Cove Cave with the largest cave opening in the state and a creek running straight through it. Do note that this trail is rated as challenging and the cave is often closed to protect the bats.

Heading east from the visitor center on Hwy 41S leads to the Grundy Lakes and Foster Falls park areas. A side road turns left off the highway to the scenic Grundy Lakes area, with its four small lakes enjoyed for fishing and swimming. The main lake, Grundy Lake, has a picnic area, a sand beach and restrooms on its east shore with another picnic area on the west shore. The other three lakes are smaller, with a paved road running around them all for easy access. A wooded hiking trail, the

Lone Rock Trail, circles for 2.3 miles around the lakes. An interesting, historic remnant to see in this part of the park are the Coke Ovens. In the 1800s, a farmer discovered coal on his property and mining operations soon developed to

South Cumberland State Park:

• Visitor Center * Camping * Hiking Trails * Lake Fishing & Swimming
* Playground * Picnic Pavilions * Tennis, Basketball, Volleyball Courts

convert the coal into more usable coke. The coal was loaded into outdoor ovens to bake into coke and many of these old ovens still stand today as a reminder of those past mining operations.

Further down Hwy 41S, a side road winds right to Foster Falls, situated in the center of the 178-acre TVA Small Wild Area. Near the falls parking lot is the only camping area in the entire South Cumberland State Park, except for primitive backcountry campsites. The Foster Falls Campground has 26 rustic sites, suitable for tents or pop-up campers, on a wooded loop road, with grills and picnic tables, restrooms with heated showers, and a nice pavilion. From the falls parking lot, an easy handicapped-accessible trail leads to a wooden overlook with fine vistas down to Foster Falls, which drops in a long 60-foot plunge into a deep pool below. For a longer hike, a five miles trail leads past several waterfalls and overlooks. Another short steep trail winds down over rocks and stairs to a suspension bridge across the river to the base of the falls where many visitors enjoying swimming in the pool.

A long drive up Hwy 56 leads to the Savage Gulf area of the park, the final section we explored on our visit. Visitors could easily spend a day or more in this area alone hiking the many trails into the Savage Creek gulf or chasm, which was named for an early settler Sterling Savage. There are four vehicular points of access in the Savage Gulf area: Greeter Falls and the Stone Door areas on the west, Collins West to the south, and Savage Gulf Campground to the east. We explored the western side of the Gulf, hiking to Greeter Falls and the Stone Door.

Not far beyond Beersheba Springs on Hwy 56, a road to the right leads back to the parking lot for Greeter Falls. Across from the parking area a sign marks the he-

ginning of the trail. The path wanders into the woods and then begins to descend over a rockier and rougher terrain, passing under overhanging bluffs and winding toward the falls area. A second sign directs hikers on toward Greeter Falls or offers a loop walk by Broadtree Falls, a long chute-falls only visible from the pathway. Continuing on to Greeter Falls soon leads to a trail split. The Upper Falls Trail on the right curls to an overlook to view Greeter Falls, for a one mile roundtrip hike. The Lower Falls Trail leads left to wind steeply down rocks, a metal spiral staircase and several levels of stairs to the base of Lower Greeter Falls. On the day we visited, the water levels were so low, that all three falls were nearly invisible.

Our exploration day ended at the Stone Door Ranger Station and Campground, a pretty place further up Hwy 56. Behind the small ranger station trails lead left to Laurel Falls and right to the Stone Door. The walk to Laurel Falls is a loop trail that drops down a steep path to a 25-foot waterfall spilling over a bluff. An overlook provides a nice spot for viewing the falls with steep stairs winding up behind the overlook to end the loop walk.

Back at the ranger station, a second trail leads in a two-miles round trip walk to the Stone Door, where a series of high rocky bluffs split to form a long slit, or door, between them. Rocky steps have been built to walk down through the door, and overlooks above the door provide beautiful vistas out over the gorge. The early part of this pathway is paved and handicapped-accessible, leading to fine views at the Laurel Gulf Overlook at 0.2 mile. After this point, the remaining 0.7 mile trail to the Stone Door is not paved. This hike was the prettiest of our day and made a fine finale to our exploration of the South Cumberland.

Cedars of Lebanon State Park

Middle Tennessee - Wilson County
Park Address: 328 Cedar Forest Road, Lebanon, TN 37090
Park Size: 900 acres   Month Visited: August
Directions: From I-40 between Nashville and Cookeville, take
Hwy 321 south to park entrance at Cedar Forest Road. Park is 10
miles south of Lebanon.

Park Description:

Clear signs off the Murfreesboro Highway point the way to the Cedars of Lebanon State Park, the developed portion of the larger Cedars of Lebanon State Forest. The park lies to the east while a 1,043 acres undeveloped section of forestland lies to the west, designated as a state natural area. The major portion of the tract is compact with its different sections easy to access.

A short distance beyond the entrance sign is the park office on the right, an interesting modern building. Inside the office visitors can pick up a park brochure, trail map, and an interesting nature guide to help identify trees, plants, wildlife, and other diverse botanical and geological formations the park is famous for. Beside the office, be sure to walk and enjoy the half-mile Cedar Glades Trail, an easy loop hike with interpretive and illustrated signs to describe the ecology and history of the area. Here you will see your first red cedars and cedar glades, silvery reindeer moss, and other unusual and endangered plants. The park and state forest are home to 350 plant species.

Down the street from the office is a picnic area with a pavilion and several picnic shelters scattered throughout it. Cedars Of Lebanon Park has three large picnic pavilions as well as many small covered shelters. Beyond the picnic area is a rustic recreation lodge, the Cedar Lodge, a popular spot for weddings and group events. Where the park road splits in front of Cedar Lodge, you will see the trail sign for

another of the park's five hiking trails. The two miles Cedar Forest Trail is a somewhat rocky trail looping back into the forest and passing many red cedar trees on its route. Next door to Cedar Lodge, which has now been placed on the National Register of Historic Places, is the Merritt Nature Center. The small museum has displays and interpretive exhibits within. A beautiful Butterfly Garden
spreads along a winding trail behind it that includes many varieties of wildflowers, rest benches, and interesting statuary.

The Dixon Merritt Trail that leads to Jackson Cave can also be found behind the center. This nice half-mile loop leads across a bridge on a scenic path to a low cave in a rocky sink area. Jackson Cave is 30 feet wide and four feet deep with an underground corridor extending approximately 1,000 feet to a pool of water. Adjacent to the nature area is a baseball field, playground, an assembly hall, and a picturesque gazebo called the Juniper Gazebo, nice for small weddings and
events. Past the recreation area are the park's two camping areas. Cedars of Lebanon has 117 campsites, 87 sites with electric and water hookups, grills, and picnic tables and 30 smaller sites for tents and pop-up campers. A large group lodge can also be found down a side road. The camping area has three bathhouses, a dump station, and a laundromat and it was full of campers on the summer day we visited. A short walk from the camping area is the park's big Olympic swimming pool with a separate children's pool and a snack bar. Beside the pool is the disc golf course, an 18-hole short Frisbee course that winds through a cedar woods. Ed Headrick, the Father of disc golf, designed this layout in 1977.

Cedars of Lebanon State Park:

• Visitor Center * Camping * Hiking Trails * Swimming Pool
* Disc Golf * Picnic Pavilions * Horse Stables & Rentals * Museum

A road to the right past the campground and pool leads to another picnic locale with many tables on a shady hill, a pavilion, and restrooms. Across from the picnic area is the Hidden Springs Trail, a five-miles trail—the longest in the park—that loops through the forest to cedar glades and a large sinkhole. At the end of the road is the Cedars of Lebanon Riding Stable. Riders can take a guided 2.5 miles trail ride that takes about 45 minutes. Locals can bring their own horses to ride here, too, if desired.

Returning back from the stable, the main road loops left to head toward the park's rental cabins, tucked under shady trees on a side road. All have nice porches and grills and are fully furnished. Beside the road to the cabins is the Limestone Sinks Trail. This half-mile trail was our favorite in the park. It loops around through the woods and beside an interesting diversity of sinks and caves. Over time, parts of the limestone dissolved or got carried away leaving cavities or caves underground. When these areas collapsed, depressions or sinks developed.

Many different sizes and kinds of sinks, cavities and small caves can be seen on the Limestone Sinks Trail. Also along the trail are big limestone rocks, many with ripples and fossils in them. This nice forest walk also passes a variety of trees and shrubs—hickory, pin oaks and post oaks, Saint-Johns-Wart with yellow flowers in the summer months, hackberries, and red cedars. We loved discovering a huge oak tree with abnormal growths on it called oak galls.

These large protruding bumps are caused by a fungus or by insects laying their eggs inside the tree's trunk.

The Cedars of Lebanon State Park is a nice park for explorations, events, picnicking, camping, and short family hikes. Because of the park's historical significance, the rangers offer many interpretive hikes and tours, especially in the summer months.

History Note:

Cedars of Lebanon Park is named for the Eastern Red Cedar trees found within the park. These are not true cedars as the Eastern Red Cedar is actually in the Juniper botanical family. However, these red cedars reminded early settlers of the cedar trees native to the Middle East including the Lebanon cedars, thus coining the name. Most of the red cedars that once densely covered the park area were destroyed by logging in the early 1900s but many remain and others are being re-introduced.

A unique limestone rock ecosystem in the park encourages the growth of red cedars and supports nineteen other endangered species of plants that don't grow anywhere else in the world. German and American botanists began to notice the ecological importance of the park areas' cedar glades in the early 1900s. In the 1930s as a part of the Lebanon Cedar Forest Project, the Works Project Administration began to

construct recreational facilities and to plant thousands of red cedar seedlings. The land was managed by the Tennessee Department of Conservation until Cedars Of Lebanon became a state park in 1955.

Bledsoe Creek State Park

Middle Tennessee - Sumner County
Park Address: 400 Zieglers Fort Road, Gallatin, TN 37066
Park Size: 169 acres   Month Visited: August
Directions: From I-40 take Hwy 231 north at Lebanon, turn left
on Hwy 25 Hartsville Pike approximately 15 miles to turn left on
Zieglers Fort Road to park

Park Description:

Bledsoe Creek State Park is a small but scenic site on a peninsula tucked
on the Bledsoe Creek embayment of Old Hickory Lake. It became a state park
in 1973. Bledsoe Creek lies in a historically significant area with many notable
homes, a former stagecoach stop, and other evidences of early settlers of the
1700s and 1800s nearby.

Every part of this charming park is easily accessible by bike, car, or a
short hike from one end to another. Bledsoe Creek is beautifully kept, neat and
clean throughout, with friendly, knowledgeable campground hosts and park staff.
Walking trails meander throughout the woods and forest and along the shoreline.
White-tailed deer and wild turkeys abound. The deer and turkeys are practically
tame, giving plenty of opportunities to enjoy watching and photographing them.
There are also spots to feed turtles and ducks and visitors will enjoy many bird
varieties both inland and on the lake including herons, egrets, and wood ducks.
In spring a wide variety of wildflowers bloom along the park trails.

A modern two-storied visitor center stands on the right of the road after
entering the park with rocking chairs on the broad back porch looking out over the
lawn and woods.   The center has nice facilities and interpretive exhibits and you
can pick up brochures and a hiking trail pamphlet with a good map inside. Close

to the visitor center are access points to two of the park's six hiking trails. Across the street from the center the High Ridge Trail begins its 1.3 miles journey up and around the forest ridges of the park, and behind the center the Mayo Wix Trail begins a 1.0 mile trek through an open woods in an easy loop walk. The first section of this pathway is paved and handicap accessible and links over to the

Birdsong Interpretive Nature Trail across the lake, which ends at one of the park's two boat ramps. The Mayo trail also winds over to a great children's playground, a picnic area and pavilion, and an open field area for entertainment events with a covered stage at its end called Bo's Picking Post.

Bledsoe Creek has 57 campsites, all level with grills and picnic tables, and the park recently added eight primitive campsites. Picnic spots are scattered throughout the park along with two pavilions, the largest near the playground area. At the end of the Bledsoe Park Road is a large parking area and a second boat ramp for entry to Old Hickory Lake, a 22,500 acres reservoir. Fishing is popular on the lake and bluegill, catfish, bass, sauger, and crappie are all caught and anglers can also enjoy nice fishing spots along the bank.

Running from the boat ramp along the side of the lake is the Shoreline Trail, which connects to other park trails to form a 2.8 miles loop walk. Other hiking trails include the short 0.25 mile Owl Ridge and the 0.20 mile Woodchuck Hollow trails. Near the trail sign for the Owl Ridge Trail is the newly completed Trade Cabin, a hand-hewn log cabin built by volunteers and staff of the park. Beside the cabin is the Long Hunter Encampment area created to commemorate the long hunters who once led hunting expeditions in the area in the 1700s.

Long Hunter State Park

Middle Tennessee - Wilson and Rutherford Counties
Park Address: 2910 Hobson Pk, Hermitage, TN 37076
Park Size: 2,600 acres   Month Visited: August
Directions: From I-40 take Hwy 171 south at Mt. Juliet to the
main park entrance.

Park Description:

Long Hunter State Park, formed in 1968, is a "long" park, beginning on J. Percy Priest Lake near the Rural Hill community and then sprawling in different, unlinked sections to the north, south, and east. The park sections are: (1) Bakers Grove to the north, (2) the main Couchville area off Hobson Pike which includes the nearby Cedar Glade area, (3) Bryant Grove, to the south off Couchville Pike, heading toward Waterhill and Murfreesboro, and (4) the Sellars Farm State Archeological Site that the park manages near Watertown, approximately 30 minutes away.

To begin exploring this park, start at the visitor center off Hobson Pike. Pick up a brochure, map, and directions to the different areas of the park and enjoy the interpretive exhibits. Beside the center is the first of twelve diverse hiking trails in Long Hunter. The easy one mile Deer Trail, noted for its wildflowers, loops through the woods to a group camp area and then back to the center. The group camp and two remote backcountry campsites are the only areas for camping in the park, but there are many picnic spots, a small scenic interior lake, the Jones Mountain Bike Trail, and a nice swim beach at Bryant Grove. In addition, many points of access for fishing and boating can be found along the 14,000

acres J. Percy Priest Lake and the park has two public boat launch ramps.

Near the visitor center are two picnic sites with fine views out over the lake and good spots for fishing or kayaking. The Inland Trail links the two areas with an 0.8 mile easy walk through the woods. Past these two locations is the Couchville Lake area, one of the most popular parts of the park. The scenic 110-acres lake is beautiful with a large picnic area and a pavilion on the lake, popular for group events. A long fishing pier reaches far into the lake with a covered deck at its end. A boat rental facility beside the pier rents canoes and jon boats. The two miles Couchville Lake Trail weaves around the perimeter of the lake, crossing a long wooden bridge and providing several nice overlooks along the lake. This paved trail is easy for all to enjoy, handicap accessible, and very picturesque.

On the north end of the park is the less-developed Bakers Grove area. Visitors will find a parking area to the left off Bakers Grove Road and the trailhead for the 4-miles Day Loop Trail. This rocky, woods trail links into the five miles Volunteer Trail that winds along the shore of J. Percy Priest Lake to a back country campsite. The park map also notes an access route to the Volunteer Trail at the other end of Bakers Grove Road but at this time it leads to a gated dead end, with a "Do Not Enter" sign and parking spaces for visitors.

Heading south on Mount Juliet Road leads by the Couchville Cedar Grove Area where the 0.8 mile Cedar Glade Trail leads through red cedars. Continuing south on Counchville Pike leads to the Bryant Grove Area, which contains several shady picnic areas, a rock pavilion on the hillside, and a popular sandy swim beach. The Bryant Grove Trail also begins here winding for four miles through the woods and along the lakeside. For an added park visit, rangers take tours to the Sellars Farm State Archeological Site to see the remains and mounds of what was once a large Native American community.

Tennessee Bicentennial Capitol Mall State Pk.

Middle Tennessee - Davidson County
Park Address: 600 James Robertson Pkwy, Nashville, TN 37243
Park Size: 19 acres   Month Visited: October
Directions: From I-40 take Broadway exit #209 in Nashville.
Turn right on Broadway into town and left on 8th Avenue/Rosa
Parks Blvd. Follow under the overpass at Capitol Hill and swing
left on Rosa Parks at the park sign. Turn right on Harrison and
drive up 6th or 7th Avenues on either side of park to look for
street parking. On weekends, you may need to park at the court-
house parking lot, a few blocks away.

Park Description:

The Bicentennial Capitol Mall
State Park sits on 19 acres of land below
Capitol Hill in downtown Nashville,
Tennessee, with the city skyline rising
all around the park. It is a busy place
at any time of day—heavily visited by
tourists and locals—and even on a fall
weekday, we were lucky to find street-
side parking. The park acreage lies in
a long rectangle between 6th and 7th
avenues, the James Robertson Parkway
to the south and Jefferson Street to the
north. The 16-acres Farmers' Market, a
part of the Bicentennial State Park Mall
development, lies to the east of the site
and is home to farmers, artisans, food
vendors, and merchants—a fun place to
explore while at the state park.

We began our journey exploring the grounds at the visitor center
under the railroad trestle at the park's
entrance. Picnic tables sit under the
railroad trestle, looking out at the lovely Rivers Of Fountain display with its
31 fountains representing the 31 waterways in the state. In this plaza also
is the colorful Tennessee state flag display. Directly behind the fountain plaza is the park's large 2,000 seat outdoor
amphitheater. To either side of the amphitheater, two long parallel sidewalks,

called the Walkway of Counties, lead down each side of the long park. Engravings in the sidewalks, along with regional vegetation along the way, celebrate the diversity of the state's 95 counties and the grounds are beautifully landscaped.

A park map, which can be picked up at the visitor center, shows where all the historic monuments and commemorative points in the park are located and a descriptive sheet describes each spot in more detail. On Wednesdays free tours are offered by park rangers and during the week, group tours can be scheduled by reservation. We spotted several school groups and bevies of internationals touring the park the day we visited.

Memorials in the Bicentennial premises include the 1,400 Wall of History on the west of the park, containing pylons engraved with historic events. These include the World War II Memorial pillars, the Centennial Memorial with its tall granite markers, and the Statehood Memorial and McNairy Spring with a pretty fountain at its centerpiece. A highlight was the World War II Memorial globe, an 18,000 pounds globe of black granite floating in a base of water. Tourists

can stop and turn the globe to view areas of the world as they existed during World War II. At the end of the park lies the Court of Three Stars and the Bell Carillon. We enjoyed listening to the bells while picnicking on a shaded bench. After all the 95 bells rang, representing the 95 counties of Tennessee, the State Capitol bell rang in answer, symbolizing the concept that the state government answers to the people of the state. This is a wonderful, scenic park to visit and one which teaches more about the State of Tennessee and its history.

Radnor Lake State Natural Area

Middle Tennessee - Davidson County
Park Address: 1160 Otter Creek Drive, Nashville, TN 37220
Park Size: 1,332 acres   Month Visited: October
Directions: From I-40 take 440 loop, exit Hillsboro Pike. Follow
Hillsboro Pike south, left on Woodmont Blvd and then right on
Granny White Pike. Watch for Otter Creek Road on the left, just
before the Grany White Market on right. There is no park sign.
Follow Otter Creek Road into the parking lot by the visitor center.

Park Description:

Radnor Lake is a sprawling city park in suburban Nashville's Oak Hill area about 15-20 minutes from downtown. The visitor center and main entrance is off Granny White Road with an alternate entrance and smaller parking area off Franklin Pike. This popular city park, closing at sunset, is always busy and finding a car space in the limited parking areas can sometimes be a challenge, especially on weekends.

The parkland, designated as a Class II State Natural area, spreads through the woodlands around Radnor Lake. The lake, created by the L&N Railroad in the early 1900s, later became a Sportsman's Club before efforts began to develop the grounds into a park. Visitors should expect to walk to see all areas of this scenic park as Otter Creek Road, running directly through the park, is closed to through traffic.

We started our park exploration at the Walter Criley Visitor Center. Visitors can find a wall size map of the park and trail system here, pick up a pocket-size map and information, and view an interesting 18 minute film on how the natural area was saved in the early 1970s. Radnor Park now has over six miles of trails and is known for its wildlife—waterfowl, reptiles, amphibians, mammals, mink, otter and a wide diversity of wildflowers, ferns, mosses, and trees. We saw an assortment of wildlife, including turtles, on the easy 1.3 miles Lake Trail that circles Radnor

Lake. The trail is mulch and gravel, even suitable for strollers, and there are several rest benches and observation points with benches along the way. From the observation decks on the lake water birds, including wintering and migrating species, can be seen in spring and fall. For more challenging hikes, Ganier Ridge Trail, 1.6 miles, rises up and over Harris Ridge, and the South Cove

Trail, 1.3 miles, winds through the forest below the South Lake Trail. In addition, several small side trails lead to points of interest. We hiked over the Spillway Bridge and Dam Walkway and then downhill on the Valve House Trail. Interpretive signs tell the story of how the railroad developed this area and explain the construction of the dam and valve house.

The park recently opened a new aviary attraction, the Barbara J. Mapp Aviary Education Center, to house birds of prey, great horned owls, and bald eagles. A 550-foot boardwalk angles through the natural area at the end of Hall Drive to the center. To minimize stress on the birds, the aviary is only open two days a week, Wednesdays and Saturdays, or for special

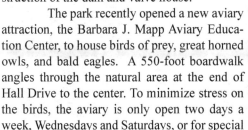

educational programs. Rangers lead informative programs at the aviary and at an outdoor amphitheater nearby. We did not visit the park on one of the aviary's open days, but you may want to plan your visit to the park on a day when the aviary is open. Radnor Park is a jewel close to downtown Nashville and has been designated as the largest pocket of wilderness in close proximity to a major city in the United States.

Tims Ford State Park

Middle Tennessee - Franklin County
Park Address: 570 Tims Ford Drive, Winchester, TN 37398
Park Size: 1,321 acres   Month Visited: November
Directions: From east Tennessee via Chattanooga, take I-24 to exit
127. Turn left onto Hwy 64 W, Veterans Memorial By-Pass. Turn
right onto Mingo Road. Take Mingo Road to a 4-way stop, turn
right onto Owl Hollow Road, then turn left at Hwy 50 W, then
right onto Munsford Rd/WR 476. Park entrance is 5 miles on the
left. From west Tennessee via Nashville, take I-24 E to exit 111 at
Manchester. Turn right onto Hwy 55 W into Tullahoma. Turn left
onto State Hwy 130 S. Follow Hwy 130 S to Awalt Rd/SR 476
and turn right. Follow Awalt Rd until it dead ends at Munsford
Rd/SR 476. Park entrance is 1.6 miles on the right.

Park Description:

Tims Ford State Park lies near the southern border of Middle Tennessee
about ten miles from Winchester. The 1,321 acres park sprawls around the borders of the beautiful Tims Ford Lake, allowing many opportunities for boating,
fishing, or just enjoying scenic vistas across the lake. Tims Ford has many amenities, all centrally located—hiking trails, a campground and cabins, picnic areas
and pavilions, a large recreational area, children's park and swimming pool, boat
ramps, marina and restaurant, and a Jack Nicklaus signature golf course. Tims
Ford Lake was created in 1970 when a dam on the Elk River was built, forming
the 10,700 acres lake with 265 miles of picturesque shoreline. The park was established in 1978.

The first stop after entering Tims Ford should be the visitor center, which
has a gift shop and park information. Many types of birds can be spotted throughout the area and some are kept in an enclosure by the visitor center. Several of the
park's nine hiking and biking trails begin near the center. The 1.2 miles Marble
Plains Loop Trail is a paved trail leading out to the Marble Plains Overlook. With
rest benches every 400 feet, it is a nice trail for all abilities and ages. Behind
118

the visitor center the 1.3 miles Lost Creek Overlook Trail begins, too, leading to two swinging bridges and another nice overlook. The first bridge, not far from the center, is a long, wooden slat bridge that sways and wobbles as you cross it—a nice spot for photos. The ongoing trail grows more strenuous and leads to a wooden deck overview, the views mostly obscured by foliage.

Across the street from the visitor center is the Old Spann House Trail. This four miles trail winds into the woods and past an area where an old homestead stood long ago, although there are no remains of the Spann house to see now. This trail crosses a few small streams on its way, ending with a loop before starting back to the trail's beginning.

Beyond the visitor center a left turn leads to the park's camping area. It has 52 RV or tent campsites, bathhouses, picnic tables, fire rings, and a disposal station—all tucked around a scenic circular road. Many of the sites offer picturesque lake views. The park has another campground, called the Fairview Campground, with an additional 82 sites, located eight miles from the main park on the lake and open seasonally from April to October.

Returning back to the main road from the camping area, the next road on the left winds down to a nice picnic area with two large, covered pavilions. Below the first pavilion, several paths connect to a shoreline hiking and biking trail and a scenic bridge that crosses an inlet of the Tims Ford Lake. This is a pretty spot, and you can bike or hike across the bridge to take the continuing trail on the other side that is a part of the 6 miles Tims Ford Bicycle Trail. Note that you cannot see the bridge from the road, but can see it from the parking lot beside the pavilion and access to it is easy.

Tims Ford State Park:

• Visitor Center * Camping * Hiking Trails * Swimming Pool *Tennis
* Fishing * Picnic Pavilions * Marina * Boat Rentals * Playground
* Bear Trace Golf Course

After returning from the loop road to the picnic area, the main road winds downhill to the park's cabins, marina, and recreation area on a peninsula of land jutting out into the lake. A road to the right leads to twenty well-appointed cabins on a quiet wooded loop road. All have a large living area, two bedrooms, with full kitchens and scenic decks overlooking the water. Not far from the cabins on a picturesque hillside is the park's recreational building, large Olympic-

sized swimming pool, snack shop, and a shaded children's park with swings and play equipment. The complex has volleyball, basketball, horseshoes, and picnic tables under the trees.

At the road's end is a boat ramp, long fishing dock, and the Lakeview Marina. Boat rentals—fishing boats, canoes, and pontoons—are available and bait and supplies can be purchased, along with gas and camping supplies. A small restaurant, called the Hard Dock Café, offers breakfast, lunch, and dinner during season, along with Saturday night music on the cafe's outside deck. The marina's convenience store also has essential groceries and snacks for those camping or visiting at the park.

In addition, a new RV Park with 30 spaces sits on a hilltop overlooking the lake and marina. Boating and fishing are popular on the lake and the expanse of the lake provides many opportunities for recreational activities. The lake is stocked with hybrid striped bass and many professional and local tournaments are conducted on Tims Ford Lake. Not far from the park on the Elk

River below the dam, anglers also enjoy fishing for rainbow and brown trout.

Across from the Lakeview Marina, another of the park's trails begins. The Clifton Doyle Trail, starting near the marina, is a 0.75 mile loop pathway hugging the shoreline around a small peninsula before curling back again. Scenic picnic tables near the trailhead look out over the lake. The entire park is latticed with over 27 miles of hiking and biking trails, and most all areas of the park are easily accessible for biking or walking. The short Highland Rim Trail is especially known for its wildflowers in the spring.

On the road returning to the visitor center, a left turn leads to the beautiful 18-hole Jack Nicklaus signature golf course. This is a lovely course laid out on a peninsula in the lake with many fine views across Tims Ford Lake. The golf course has ample parking around its large clubhouse, and inside the clubhouse is a seasonal restaurant with scenic views across the course and the lake. We had lunch there while at the park.

The Bear Trace at Tims Ford has received widespread acclaim and was cited as one of the "Best New Destinations" in Tennessee in 1999 and one of the "Top Ten Places You Can Play" by *Golf Magazine* in 2000. The course has a 6,763 yard layout with undulating greens and a true tournament feel.

Old Stone Fort State Archaeological Park

Middle Tennessee - Coffee County
Park Address: 732 Stone Fort Drive, Manchester, TN 37355
Park Size: 2,875 acres   Month Visited: November
Directions: From I-40 near Cookeville, exit on Hwy 56 south
through Smithville and to McMinnville. At McMinnville, take
Hwy 55 into Manchester. Cross Interstate 24 and then turn north
on Hwy 41E to Stone Fort Drive and the park entrance on the left.
From I-24, take Hwy 53 exit at Manchester, right on 41E to Stone
Fort Drive to park entrance.

Park Description:

Old Stone Fort State Archaeological Park is an ancient Indian enclosure. The primary historic acreage of the park sits on a hilltop peninsula of land enclosed by the Duck River and Little Duck River. A name like Old Stone Fort leads visitors to expect a fort—some kind of tall building or enclosure made of wood or stone. The fort's walls instead are only four to six feet tall in most places, constructed of piled stone covered with earth on a 50 acres plateau. Early historians believed the old walled structure had been created for use as a fortification by early explorers or possibly as a military outpost—thus the park's name. However, in 1966, a group of archaeologists from the University of Tennessee found evidence showing the structure was built instead between 80 AD and 550 AD over 2,000 years ago by Native American peoples during the Middle Woodland Period. It is now believed the site was utilized more for sacred ceremonies, but its site would have been well chosen for fortification safety as well. One of two archaeological

parks in Tennessee, Old Stone Fort State Archaeological Park is listed on the National Register of Historic Places.

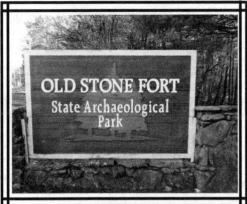

The old area is steeped in history. Accounts of early visits to a little known cave in the 19th Century described the discovery of large human skeletons. These were found in an ancient cavern underneath the park, leading to the nickname of "Bone Cave." The entire area is latticed with caves although none are featured in the park.

Industry thrived in the area in earlier times. Samuel Murray built a rope factory on the Little Duck River in 1823 and W. S. Whitman built a paper mill on the Duck River before the Civil War along with a gunpowder mill. After the war Whitman sold his property to the Wooten and Hickerson families who expanded the mill into the Stone Fort Paper Mill. The mill supplied paper to many businesses and newspapers around the Southeast, including *The Nashville Banner* and *Atlanta Constitution*, until its close in the 1930s when the property passed hands to the Chumbley family. Remnants of the old mill can still be found on the park grounds near Big Falls

on the Duck River. In 1966, when the archaeological significance of the park was discovered, the state purchased acreage from the Chumbley estate and established the core portion of the park, adding land to the state park grounds later on.

Entering the park on Old Stone Drive leads along a winding, shady woods road, occasionally skirting the Duck River, before the road reaches a loop turnaround and parking area near the visitor center and museum. Along the way,

we crossed the Duck River on a historic green metal bridge, clacking over the old wooden boards, to get to the park's campground. The park has 51 campsites, restrooms, and a dump station but it might be wise to check with the park about the size and weight of RVs that can safely cross the narrow bridge into the campground area.

Fishing is popular with anglers by boat and along the banks of the Duck River. There is no boat ramp at Old Stone Fort Park but access to the river can be made at public boat ramps at nearby sites like Cedar Point Boat Dock and Public Use Area, the Wards Chapel Public Boat Ramp, and the Barton Spring Public Use Area in Manchester. The park office can provide advice and suggestions.

Two of the park's hiking trails, the 0.9 mile Garrison Road Trail and the one mile Nature Trail begin near the campground area. The park has seven trails and dogs are welcome in Old Stone Fort on leash. The Old Stone Fort Loop Trail is the most hiked trail, passing historic sites and waterfalls.

The two miles Golf Course Trail lies near the Old Stone Fort Golf Course, a 9-hole course that used to be owned by the state and was a part of the state park system. The course is on Country Club Road behind the park and was recently purchased by Driver Properties and reopened as a public course. The course grounds were once hunting and ceremonial grounds for Native Americans and golfers enjoying the course might still spot deer and wild turkeys.

Continuing on the main road into the park and past a playground and picnic area leads to a parking area at the road's end. A walkway to the right winds around to the museum and park office. The museum is a beautiful, old stone structure beside the Duck River with a patio and overlook on top of it. Inside the museum are a visitor center with maps and information about the park, an interpretive film, a small museum, dioramas, historical photos, and a gift shop. Behind the museum the 1.3 miles long Old Stone Fort Enclosure Trail begins, making a loop through the archaeological site and back to the museum. The entrance to the old Indian complex starts between two large earthen, grassy mounds, which align to the sunrise on the day of the summer solstice. In many areas along the trail, signs explain points along the pathway, facts about the Indian culture that once lived here, or point out sections of the old earthen wall built thousands of years ago—with remnants still left behind.

On the left the trail soon follows along the high bank above the Little Duck River. Step Falls is soon visible from several overlooks along the path. The trail drops off steeply on the left. It is easy to see how the high ridges and gorges dug out by the river created a natural, safe enclosure for the ancient Indian site. After a walk through the woods, the trail opens out into a wide field near where the Duck River and Little Duck River meet. Several other park trails branch off from this area, the short 0.4 mile Forks in the River Trail, the 0.6 mile Abandoned River Channel Trail and the longer 1.5 miles Little Duck Loop Trail that winds down to a peninsula of the Little Duck River.

Curling around and starting back toward the museum, the trail now moves alongside the Duck River on the west side of the Indian enclosure. This section of the trail is more open with vistas to some of the old walls of the enclosure and across the river. Pretty view points and overlooks peek down over deep river pools and across Big Falls as it cascades over the rocks. Further along a pathway leads down to the remains of the old mill, an interesting spot to explore. Nearby is beautiful Bluehole Falls, spanning across the river, created to divert the river into the old mill. The trail ends again at the museum, a nice time to climb up to the overlook on top to look out over the river a last time.

Henry Horton State Park

Middle Tennessee - Marshall County
Park Address: 4209 Nashville Hwy, Chapel Hill, TN 37034
Park Size: 1,523 acres   Month Visited: April
Directions: From I-40 east of Nashville, take the 840 Highway
Loop swinging south of Nashville. Exit onto Hwy 41/31 south,
and stay on Hwy 31 at the road split. Continue south on Hwy 31
through Chapel Hill and look for park signs as the highway travels
through the park.

Park Description:

Henry Horton State Park is an interesting state park split in half by the
busy Nashville Highway. The 1,532 acres park, created in the 1960s, was built
on the estate of the former governor of Tennessee, Henry Horton. Horton was
the 36th Tennessee governor from 1927 to 1933. He moved to Marshall County
with his wife Adeline to help manage his wife's family's farm and the Wilhoite
grain and lumber mill on the Duck River, all a part of the state park today. The
governor's beautiful antebellum home was torn down during construction of the
park but the family cemetery, where Henry, Adeline, and many of their family
members are buried, still stands on park property by the Nashville Highway.

The visitor center is located on Park Road, which loops around the main
park. The road travels by the Henry Horton Inn, Governor's Table Restaurant,

Tipped Canoe snack bar and lounge, Conference Lodge, Olympic pool and recreation area, and rental cabins. Along the Park Road by the Duck River are scenic picnic tables and three lovely pavilions, nice for family events. On the back of Park Road is a paved access road leading down to the river for small boats like canoes or kayaks. This is also the beginning point for the Blueway Trail, a one mile paddle trail in the Duck River.

Within this main section of the park are playground areas for kids, volleyball and basketball courts, and a disc golf course. The Olympic-sized swimming pool, with a separate wading pool and concessions snack bar, is a favorite spot in the summer months. Not far from the pool is a quiet quarter mile Greenway Trail loop, paved for easy walking for all ages, with markers to identify trees and plants. In the middle of the park is a field of native grasslands and a big vegetable garden.

The Henry Horton Inn is a popular venue for conferences and events with 68 rooms, four large meetings rooms, and a boardroom. In addition, the Conference Lodge, in a separate building, can host meetings for larger groups. The park also has three well-equipped rental cabins near the inn and restaurants.

Returning to the main highway and driving south a few blocks leads to a second section of the park where Warner Road travels to the archery range and skeet and trap range, well removed from the main park areas. This shooting range, one of the finest in the state, has five skeet fields and two trap fields with skeet, trap, wobble trap, and five stand shooting. Rental guns and ammo are available as well as a concessions area. The shooting range is not open year round, so check with the park for hours. Also on Warner Road is another of the park's hiking trails, the Wild Turkey Trail, a two miles loop trail, winding back into the woods. Two turkeys greeted us at the trail entrance the day

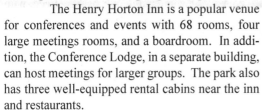

Henry Horton State Park:

• Visitor Center * Camping * Hiking Trails * Swimming Pool * Biking
* Fishing * Picnic Pavilions * Restaurant * Conference Lodge * RV Sites
* Buford Ellington Golf Course * Henry Horton Inn * Skeet Range

we visited the park, a hen and a male gobbler, who fanned out his feathers, showing off for the hen—and perhaps for us.

Across the Nashville Highway from the main park area is the Buford Ellington Championship golf course, named for another of Tennessee's governors, who like Horton, was also a resident of Marshall County and an avid golfer. The 18-hole, par 72 championship course, is a challenging one, heavily treed, with 37 bunkers and very large greens, with a fine pro shop and a driving range.

Across the highway bridge, passing over the Duck River, are two more sections of the Henry Horton State Park. The River Road leads back into the park's campground area and to several hiking trails. The main campground area, on a quiet loop road, has 56 RV camp-sites with additional tent sites and backcountry camp areas. The campground has a check-in area, bathhouses, an amphitheater in the woods, and a large playground with a creekside pavil-ion and open playing field. Three of the park's trails, The Hickory Ridge Loop Trail, Adeline Wilhoite River Trail, and the Westland Trail can be found in this section of the park. At the back of the Wilhoite trail is an observation tower offering views of native grasslands, wetlands, and the Duck River. On all the ten miles of hiking trails in the park many species of birds, plants, and flowers can be seen.

128

Immediately across the Nashville Highway from the campground is another historic section of the state park. Here early explorers first crossed the Duck River and later other settlers, like the Wilhoite family, established farms and homes. The Wilhoite family also built the first dam and bridge on the river and they founded and ran the first water-powered grist mill and lumber mill, which operated until the 1900s.

Several trails in the park are named for the Wilhoites, like the Wilhoite Mill Trail that begins at the park area and loops through the woods and along the Duck River. Near the highway bridge you will find traces of the old mill, which operated for over a century, including a large, round pulley, a part of mill machinery that helped to grind grain at the grist mill and cut lumber.

Biking is popular in all the paved areas of the park and Henry Horton Park serves as the starting point and host for a 2-day 100 miles bike ride each year in April, called the Horton 100, popular with biking enthusiasts around the region. The park also holds other seasonal programs and activities, like the Step Back in Time Festival in September with music, old time demonstrations,

and crafters. Henry Horton State Park is convenient to find and not far from major metropolitan areas in Middle Tennessee, offering many amenities.

Montgomery Bell State Park

Middle Tennessee - Dickson County
Park Address: 1020 Jackson Hill Road, Burns, TN 37029
Park Size: 3,850 acres   Month Visited: April
Directions: Coming from east toward Nashville, take the 840 Loop
and turn west on I-40 at loop end. From I-40 take Dickson Exit
#172 onto Highway 46. Travel north on Hwy 46 to Hwy 70 and at
sign to the park turn right and follow to park entrance.

Park Description:

     A popular and beloved park, Montgomery Bell State Park sits right in the middle of Tennessee not far from Metropolitan Nashville and seven miles from Dickson. The 3,850 acres park offers something for everyone with lakes, camping and picnic areas, boating, hiking, swimming, and golf.

     Entering the park on Jackson Hill Road soon leads to the visitor center on the right. A large "Iron Man" statue stands prominently in front of the center reminding visitors that Montgomery Bell was once an early site of the iron ore industry. The park is named for the best-known iron industrialist of the 1800s era, Montgomery Bell, who was known as "The Iron Master of Middle Tennessee" and said to be the richest man in the south before the Civil War. Inside the visitor center is a small museum, gift shop, and program area.

     Behind the visitor center's parking area is the beginning of one of the park's hiking trails, the 0.75 mile Jim Bailey Nature Trail, a pretty walkway

curling along Four Mile Creek. There are 20 miles of hiking trails and many crisscross and circuit the grounds' perimeter. Across Highway 70 from the main park area, are 20 miles of mountain bike trails, ranked from easy to expert in skill level, that wind through a wooded terrain.

Traveling beyond the visitor center on Jackson Hill Road leads to the main camping area. At a check-in station, quiet roads loop through the campground offering 94 campsites, suitable for RVs and pop-ups, with other locations for tent and primitive camping. The camp sites on the back of the campground lie along Hall Creek and to the left of the camp area is a pavilion, playground, and an open playing field for games, baseball, and other outdoor sports.

The Civilian Conservation Corps (CCC) built many of the rock structures in the camp and their handiwork shows in the bridge leading back to two of the camp's historic areas. A side road leads to the site of the first Cumberland Presbyterian Church in Tennessee, founded in 1810 and pastored by Rev. Samuel McAdow. Visitors can tour a replica of the church and McAdow's log cabin and see monuments dedicated to the origins of this Christian denomination, started during "The Great Revival

Montgomery Bell State Park:

* Visitor Center * Conference Center * Montgomery Bell Inn * Restaurant
* Camping/RV * Picnic * Boating * Fishing * Cabin Rentals * Hiking
* Swimming * Frank G. Clement Golf Course

of 1800." Links into the Montgomery Bell Trail and the beginning of the Ore Pit Trail start out of this area, and picnic tables and a covered pavilion sit along the Jackson Hollow Creek, nice for family gatherings. Not far beyond the historic church area is Group Camp I, on Lake Woodhaven, with 34 cabins, a dining hall, and a nice boat dock. This early group camp is considered a historic site because

many of the rustic cabins were constructed of hand-hewn stone by the CCC workers.

The next side road off Jackson Hill Road leads to a picnic area and pavilion overlooking Woodhaven Lake. This is a scenic spot high on a hillside with fine views of the lake and the rushing spillway dam built by the CCC. A concrete walkway leads to an overlook near the dam and another link of the Montgomery Bell Trail winds out behind the pavilion. An unpaved, rough side road, further down Jackson Hill Road, leads to Group Camp II and a boat launch point on the lake with trail access to two of the park's backcountry shelters. For more hiking pleasure, several trails lead out of the group camp. Off the main road the Creech Hollow Trail travels down through the forest to Creech Hollow Lake, tucked away from the busier part of the camp and a great spot for fishing.

Returning back to the split in the road near the visitor center, Hotel Road leads to the conference center, restaurant, golf course, and the park's third lake, Acorn Lake. A picnic area and eight rental villas lie on side roads off Hotel Road, the villas modern ones with two bedrooms and two baths. As Hotel Road curls left, it passes the entry road to the Frank G. Clement Golf Course, a nationally recognized 18 hole, par-72 course. The course has a practice green, driving range, a beautiful clubhouse, snack bar, and outdoor patio.

Beyond the golf course Hotel Road splits, one road leading to the boat dock and swim area and the other to the conference center. Following the split down to the dock travels to a lovely access point on Lake Acorn. Picnic tables, a big pavilion, and snack bar overlook the lake and boat dock, with a large swimming area and beach below it. In summer, kayaks, canoes, paddleboats, and small fishing boats can be rented, and anglers love to fish along the lake banks. The Wildcat Trail

begins beside the boat dock and there is a backcountry Wildcat Shelter at the west end of the lake.

At the end of the second split of Hotel Road is the Montgomery Bell Inn and Conference Center and the Forge Restaurant, located inside the inn. The inn features 120 lake view guestrooms, a swimming pool, exercise room, and a variety of well-equipped meeting rooms, popular for conferences or social gatherings of all sizes. The restaurant, with glorious open views out over the lake, is open year round, with buffet options in the park's busier seasons. Several walking trails wind along the lake and a walkway bridge links the inn to the boat dock and swim area.

Montgomery Bell is a gem in the state park system and is busy year round. The park abounds with birds and on the Bluebird Trail are 31 nest boxes. Hummingbird feeders can be found at many points around the area and the park rangers conduct hummingbird bandings and talks, lead hikes, and give educational programs. Also 50 different species of butterflies have been documented in the park and a diversity of trees and flowers abound. This is a beautiful state park to visit.

Harpeth River State Park

Middle Tennessee - mainly Cheatham County
Park Address: 1640 Cedar Hill Road, Kingston Springs, TN 37082
Park Size: 9 access sites along 40 river miles Month Visited: April
Directions: From I-40 just west of Nashville, take exit #196 near
Bellevue area onto Hwy 70. Travel northwest on Hwy 70 through
Pegram. After crossing Hwy 249 and passing two kayak and
canoe rental stores, turn right on Cedar Hill Road and travel to the
northern most point of the park at the Harris Street Bridge.

Park Description:

     The Harpeth River State Park is unique among Tennessee's state parks.
Rather than its acreage being in one main area, this park is spread out in segments
along a 40 miles stretch of the Harpeth River from the Harris Street Bridge on
two-lane Cedar Hill Road to the Coley Davis segment near State Hwy 100 in
Nashville's Bellevue area. Harpeth River is termed a linear park and the state
system manages nine river access sites along a twisting, twining stretch of the
Harpeth River. A major tributary of the Cumberland River, the Harpeth River

is designated as a "scenic river" under the Tennessee Scenic Rivers Act. The river is especially
popular with kayakers, canoeists, and anglers.
     We started our exploration of the differ-
ent parts of this river park at its northern most
end at the Harris Street Bridge segment. A cut-
off road before the bridge travels downhill to a
gravel parking area. A few picnic tables sit along
the river with views of the bridge and just downstream is a nice access point for boaters. Beginning near the parking area, the 0.3 mile Harris
Street Bridge Trail runs along the Harpeth River,
offering a quiet walk.
     Not far from the Harris Street Bridge,
signs lead into the Narrows of the Harpeth section of the park. This area lies in a curve of the

river called Bells Bend. This is an especially pretty section of the park. The parking area sits alongside the Harpeth River with views down the river in both directions. Boaters and anglers can access the water at several points and two interesting trails begin not far from the parking area.

We especially enjoyed our half-mile walk on the Tunnel Trail. This led to the rock tunnel where Montgomery Bell's iron workers once cut through 200 yards of solid rock to divert the water flow to power his iron mill. Water pours through the tunnel in a beautiful waterfall and the diversion tunnel is considered a Historic Civil Engineering Landmark. Off the Tunnel Trail another Bluff Overlook Trail climbs up a stair-step path to travel one-third mile to a high rocky bluff with a panoramic view of the valley.

The Narrows of the Harpeth area is also known for the Mound Bottom Archaeological site, which can be seen in part across the Harpeth River at the Narrows. It looks much like a green field to most, but it once housed a prehistoric Native American complex with habitation areas and burial grounds. The Mound and nearby Pack Site contain about 34 earthen mounds, 11 to 14 at Mound Bottom. The Mound site is not open to the public but guided tours are available by request from the park.

Leaving the Narrows of the Harpeth area, we traveled back down Cedar Hill Road to the Gossett Tract segment of the park. Near the parking area, a trail leads down to an access point on the river for boaters. Behind the park area is a grassy field and several trails start nearby behind an old gate. A half-mile path called the Upper Loop Trail winds through a wildflower meadow in a wide loop. A longer one mile Lower Loop Trail curls and leads to picnic tables along the Harpeth River, continuing along the river to eventually loop back to interconnect the original trail

and return again to the parking area. Both trails are popular with locals and the wildflowers in the meadow are often a show.

We found the next Hidden Lake segment of the Harpeth River State Park off Highway 70 on McCrory Lane. A sign on Hwy 70 alerts you to the turn to locate the parking area for Hidden Lake. A kiosk tells some of the history of the park with a trail map. A short path to the left of the parking area drops down to a boat access area on the Harpeth River with a short trail winding nearby through a field.

Behind the kiosk, another trail, called the Blue Bird Loop Trail, journeys through a broad meadow and around in a circle. At the back of the Blue Bird Loop, the Hidden Lake Trail travels to the remains of the Hidden Lake Resort, a popular destination in the 1930s and 1940s. The Hidden Lake Trail, approximately a half-mile in length, winds back through the woods, past a smaller lake, then up a ridge with views of the larger Hidden Lake. At one point, the trail comes to an intersection, the left trail staying on the Hidden Lake Trail and the right climbing up the Ridge Loop Trail to reach the lake on its other side. Both trails can be linked for a longer hike, but for a shorter and easier walk, continuing on the Hidden Lake Trail reaches the old resort site sooner.

A working limestone quarry existed in the Hidden Lake area in the late 1800s to early 1900s. When the Dobson family built the resort, they turned the flooded, abandoned quarry into a recreational lake. The site was a highly popular resort with swimming in the lake, a white sand beach, dances, barbeques, a water slide and a big

waterwheel, all built around a rustic lodge. Many bands of the Big Band era played at the Hidden Lake Resort and because of its isolated location, tucked between two bluffs, some sources said it was also a popular spot for gamblers and bootleggers. The site around the old re-

sort is fun to explore and visitors can discover remains of the old concrete dance floor, a partially buried tanker, tumble down sheds and structures along with fossils in the rocks, deer, flowers, and mushrooms. Many trail books call this trail one of Tennessee's best, hidden trails.

Our final stop on our exploration trip of the Harpeth River State Park was at the Newsom's Mill river segment. Following McCrory Road almost to Interstate 40, a park sign points to a side road to the old mill, just below the Danny Tomlinson Bridge over the Harpeth River. The old 1862 Newsom's Mill ruins still stand alongside the river, once the hub of a busy community called Newsom's Station. A short trail from the parking area leads to the former grist mill. Visitors can walk around the mill and look inside at remaining machinery on the inside of the millhouse. The original mill, built by William B. Newsom in the late 1700s, was one of the first in the U.S. to have its mill works inside a housed structure, and the mill is now on the National Register of Historic Places. A small pathway winds along the river nearby and there are some picnic tables near the parking area. From the mill, it is only a short distance to return to Interstate 40.

Johnsonville State Historic Park

Middle Tennessee - Humphreys County
Park Address: 90 Nell Beard Road, New Johnsonville, TN 37134
Park Size: 1,075 acres   Month Visited: May
Directions: From I-40, west of Nashville, take Hwy 13 north to
Waverly; turn west on Hwy 70 for approximately ten miles to sign
for park on right.

Park Description:

     The Johnsonville State Historic Park memorializes the site of the historic town of Johnsonville and the Johnsonville Depot that existed from 1864 to 1944. Johnsonville, named for Andrew Johnson, was a thriving railroad town for 80 years before being flooded by water with the construction of the Kentucky Dam in 1944. Many of the town's residents moved nearby to create a new community they called New Johnsonville, incorporated in 1949. The park also commemorates the memory of the Civil War Battle of Johnsonville. During the Civil War (1861-1865) the railroad that ran from Nashville to Johnsonville on the banks of the Tennessee River provided a major supply depot for Union troops. In 1864 Confederate soldiers, led by Confederate Major General Nathan B. Forrest, attacked and defeated the Union forces holding the depot. Around the wooded grounds on the Tennessee River are many actual and recreated sites of this historic battle in the Civil War.

Although this is predominantly a historical park, recreational opportunities also exist for those who simply want to enjoy the beauty of this scenic area on the banks of the Tennessee River. The park has picnic tables and grills, ten miles of maintained hiking trails, and swimming and fishing are allowed from the bank. Water birds and wildlife are frequently seen in the area, along with a wide variety of flowers and trees.

The best place to begin an exploration of the park is at the visitor and welcome center located on Nell Beard Road. Picking up a map from the welcome center helps to pinpoint the historic spots around the grounds that visitors can see. In the center are a museum, theater, and gift shop. The original photos and artifacts in the museum, and the free film offered in the center's meeting room, highlight the earlier historic period of the Civil War, before the dam was constructed. Reenactments of the Battle of Johnsonville are held at the park during the year, along with a variety of interpretive programs, talks, and walking tours, to help bring the area's history to life.

After leaving the visitor center, follow Nell Beard Road to the Old Johnsonville Road and into the main portion of the park. At the first parking lot on the right, stop and explore the big cannon and soldiers' barracks. A row of soldiers' huts has been recreated similar to the type Union soldiers stayed in at the Johnsonville Depot. Many of the soldiers stationed at the depot were freed slaves in the 100th Unit-

ed States Colored Troops division. An African-American cemetery lies nearby where many of these soldiers are buried. A half-mile path winds up the hill to the cemetery from the parking lot. This loop trail also travels along the borders of Trace Creek, a bay of water jutting off the Tennessee River .

Continuing down the main road leads to the loop point where the railroad engines used to turn around to head back toward Nashville before meeting the Tennessee River. At the museum, we learned about many efforts after the Civil War to build railroad bridges across the Tennessee River. The first bridge across the river, built in 1867, was called the Johnsonville Railroad Bridge. It was a timber Howe truss bridge and had to be rebuilt or modified many times, but it allowed growth of the city with the railroad able to finally cross the Tennessee River rather than having to turn around and head back. The bridge had a swing section near the Eva side, across from Johnsonville, that could swing away to allow a steamboat to pass through. The Hickman-Lockhart Bridge down river near New Johnsonville on Highway 70 is a modern wonder compared to this first bridge constructed at Johnsonville. Support structures of the early Johnsonville Railroad Bridge can still be seen near the river and out in the bay on a small island.

A remnant of the historic Reynoldsburg Road walks out on a long spit of land between Trace Creek and the Tennessee River. Nearby Reynoldsburg was once an important shipping point on the Tennessee River in Humphreys County, not far from the old town of Johnsonville. Reynoldsburg on the Tennessee was where plantation owners sent their cotton for shipment and many wagon trains traveled to this old port.

Park visitors will find beautiful views out over the Tennessee River at the end of the Old Johnsonville Road and more historical markers about the Civil

War battle that happened here. The Lower Redoubt Trail wanders down the banks of the Tennessee to some old Rifle Pits and back in a loop to the park area again. Another shorter trail leads from the park's picnic area to the Rifle Pits.

More historic sites are found on the road to the park's scenic lookout. The road climbs uphill to a wooden overlook, providing high views out over the Tennessee River. Across from the overlook are more Union Rifle Pits from which Union soldiers fired on advancing troops. This road also leads to the Crockett Cemetery, founded in 1880 on a high point safe from flooding. Many early Johnsonville families are buried here, although many of the graves were never marked. In 1987, the families of those with relatives buried at the Crockett Cemetery erected a monument listing the family names of early settlers buried in the cemetery. Two park trails also begin in this area, the two miles Civil War Forts Trail and the eight miles long Historic Johnsonville Trail.

History Note:

This park is rich in history, both of the Civil War period, and of the town of Johnsonville that was later covered

with water when the Kentucky Dam was built in 1944. We enjoyed learning about the history of Johnsonville, which grew up alongside the Union supply depot on the Tennessee River. The town continued for eighty years. Civilians operated boarding houses, hotels, saloons, general stores and a variety of other businesses. Many soldiers who had served at the depot settled in the town of

Johnsonville after the Civil War, continuing the city's growth. Former soldiers farmed or worked in area businesses, and the river supported commercial fishing and musseling. The town also became a stopping point for travelers. Many local residents operated ferries or steamboats to navigate the Tennessee River, like the old sepia photo shows.

Dunbar Cave State Park

Middle Tennessee - Montgomery County
Park Address: 401 Dunbar Cave Road, Clarksville, TN 37403
Park Size: 110 acres   Month Visited: June
Directions: From I-40, take I-24 above Nashville north toward
Clarksville. Exit on Hwy 327 Rossview Road and follow to Hwy
374 Warfield Boulevard. Turn south on Warfield Blvd and to the
Dunbar Cave Road intersection. Turn west on Dunbar Cave Road
and follow to park.

Park Description:

Dunbar Cave State Park is located about one and a half miles northeast of Clarksville, Tennessee. The picturesque park is well loved by locals and tourists for its walking trails along manmade Swan Lake and for the cave. Inside the visitor center is a small museum where tourists can pick up a map of the park, information about Dunbar Cave's history, and brochures about native flowers, shrubs, trees, and dragonflies. Behind the visitor center is a large patio looking out over a flower garden, popular for group events. Markers help to identify the flowers and plants, and walkways weave through the garden to picnic tables in a shady area near the lake and the trail to the cave.

Dunbar Cave is a vast cave, measuring over eight miles in length and listed as the 280th largest cave complex in the world. In front of the cave is a large concrete structure with three distinct arches. Behind it, a wide concrete patio under a high rocky face leads to the cave entrance. Visitors can see into the cave at a gated entrance and can take scheduled tours by reservation, led by park rangers, in May, June, and July. Inside the cave, with the temperature at a cool 58 degrees, are three large caverns, an underground stream and several large pools. The cave is the habitat for rare fish, reptiles, cave crickets, amphibians like blind salamanders, and tri-colored bats.

The paved 0.67 mile Lake Trail leads to the entrance of Dunbar Cave in an easy walk.

The cave was first inhabited by prehistoric peoples and later used by Native American Indians for ceremonial purposes. Prehistoric art can be seen in the cave, dating back to 10,000 to 8,000 BC. By the 1700s, European settlers began to arrive in the area and the cave and land were claimed by Thomas Dunbar in 1784. Due to incorrect paperwork, Dunbar lost the land to surveyor Robert Nelson, but the cave retained his name and

Dunbar lived nearby until his death. In ensuing years, the cave was used to mine gunpowder and saltpeter and then developed for tourism with cabins and a hotel constructed. Many social events, dances, and concerts were held at the cave, and in 1948 singer Roy Acuff bought the property, adding a golf course and making the property an even more popular site for musical shows and entertainment. Ownership of the property passed to the King family in 1963 and in 1973 Governor Winfield Dunn bought it for a state natural area.

Near the back parking area, two more hiking trails lead into the park's property, the 1.1 miles Short Loop Trail, a moderate, easy walk linking to the longer Lake Trail, and the 1.9 miles Recovery Trail, with several steep hills. At our visit the 15 acres Swan Lake—usually a highlight of a Dunbar Cave visit—was nearly dry but the state is in process of repairing the spillway and dam, with the lake to reopen soon. The cave and park are interesting to see.

Port Royal State Historic Park

Middle Tennessee - border Montgomery and Robertson Counties
Park Address: 3300 Old Clarksville Hwy, Adams, TN 37010
Park Size: 26 acres   Month Visited: June
Directions: From I-40, take I-24 above Nashville north toward
Clarksville. Take Exit 11 east on Hwy 76 at Clarksville, then north
on Hwy 238 Port Royal Road to park.

Park Description:

The town of Port Royal, founded in 1797, began as a trading post and early colonial community. It was the only area stop on the "Great Western Road" stagecoach line and an important trading center on the Red River for settlers. From 1838 to 1839, the town also served as a resupply station and stopover point on the Trail of Tears for the Cherokee Indians. In visiting the park, foundations of stores, bridges, homes, old warehouses, and roads can be found dating back to the 18th century.

The old 1859 lodge and general store sits on the left side of the road just inside Port Royal State Historic Park beside the Red River. Behind the lodge and store is a large parking lot, restroom facilities, and a picnic area. The brick two-storied building served many purposes over its life as lodge, store, post office, telephone exchange, and site for Masonic and town meetings and local trials. When Port Royal became a state park in 1977, the state restored the old building, abandoned for years and almost in ruins. The lodge is the only remaining building from Port Royal's early history and served as the park's visitor center in past. Today, Port Royal is managed by the staff at nearby Dunbar Cave State Park and the lodge is only opened for special events.

Adjacent to the old lodge is a set of wooden stairs climbing down to the short Overlook Trail along the Red River. Picnic tables sit under the trees and a walk to the edge of the river leads to rock remains that once supported the original 1904 covered bridge over the Red River, only a short distance from the new bridge.

Port Royal Park continues across the road. Here a walkway drops from the parking lot to the river bank, a popular spot for kayaking, canoeing and swimming. Picnic tables sit nearby along a shady hillside and a path winds back along Sulphur Fork Creek to an old steel bridge. Built in 1887, this Pratt Truss design bridge was one of the first bridges built by William Converse. The trail along the river loops through an area that was once the town's Old Main Street with Port Royal site markers and historic remains.

Across the Red River and further up the road is a second parking area at the official site of the Trail of Tears. An interpretive kiosk tells some of the history of the eleven involuntary detachments of Cherokee Indians that came through Port Royal on the journey west to Oklahoma territory. A marker notes part of the original section of the Trail of Tears, an easy 0.2 mile walk. The half-mile River Bottom Trail begins out of this area, also, looping through the woods and alongside the Red River with many good fishing points.

An interesting place to stop, across from the park, is at the Port Royal General Store and Cafe. The picturesque, old country store is a great place for lunch while visiting the park. Tables on the porch look out over the area and an old cabin on the grounds was often used when reenactments, crafts fairs, and events were held in the field beside it.

Mousetail Landing State Park

Middle Tennessee - Perry County
Park Address: 3 Campground Road, Linden, TN 37096
Park Size: 1,247 acres   Month Visited: June
Directions: From I-40, take Exit 143 and travel south on Hwy 13.
Follow Hwy 13 south for 19 miles to Linden. Turn right/west on
Hwy 412 and travel 12 miles to Hwy 438 Spring Creek Road to
park entrance.

Park Description:

Established in 1986, Mousetail Landing State Park is one of the newer parks in the state park system. Located on 1,247 acres on the east banks of the Tennessee River, the park offers many amenities on the river and around the scenic Spring Creek embayment including hiking, camping, swimming, fishing, boating, and other recreational pleasures. The odd name of the park dates back to the 1800s when a tannery was located at a river landing on the site. The old tannery was infested with a huge population of mice, which fled in droves toward the landing when the tannery caught fire, inspiring the name Mousetail Landing. The community of Mousetail Landing was also a prominent river village in the 1800s and archeological ruins can be found on the grounds including the original landing pier, a cemetery, and remnants of a blacksmith shop.

The main road into the park wanders through the woods and across a small creek, a great place for children to wade and play. It then passes by one of

the park's nice recreation and playground areas. The homey visitor center sits on a hill not far from the main entrance. Informational materials about the area, brochures, and a hiking/ bike trail map are available at the office.

Near the visitor center beside the playground area is the entrance to the park's longest hiking trail. The 8.4 miles Eagle Point Overnight Trail leads in a long loop back into the park to travel along Lick Creek, the Tennessee River, and beside Parrish Branch before continuing around to its starting point. The fine trail, well-blazed and easy to walk in its entirety, follows the creek and then wanders up and down hills on its route through the park. It crosses several creeks on nice bridges with some amazing views of the river. An overnight can be planned at Shelter #1 along the way or at Shelter #2 by the river. Both shelters are enclosed, screened, and well maintained and have wire bunks, a fire ring, and a picnic table. The Eagle Point trail can also easily be walked as a day hike, although there are some steep uphill passages along its route.

Swinging to the right from the office leads into a loop road circling through the main part of the park. The primary campground lies along this road with 25 campsites, a bathhouse, a laundromat, and dump station. Twenty-one primitive campsites are also located on the other side of Spring Creek on the river. Down the road from the campground is an archery range and a side road leading to the Old Spring Picnic Shelter tucked on a shady spot on the hillside. Beyond the shelter on the right is another playground and picnic area and a short trail to the old Parrish Cemetery. The cemetery lies in a cedar grove and has over 100 marked and unmarked graves dating from the 1800s, many from the Parrish family. One interesting gravestone in the

cemetery reads: "He is not dead but only sleeping." The recreation area is a pretty one along the creek with picnic tables and a large playground. Mousetail Landing also has a baseball diamond and a volleyball court.

The paved road becomes gravel after the recreation area as it loops along the Tennessee River, but the park has recently improved the road for easy accessibility. It leads to several nice spots with picnic tables and fine views across the Tennessee River and then to a large pavilion as the gravel road merges into the

paved road again. In summer, outdoor movies and family activities are held at the pavilion and the facility can be rented for group events.

Below the pavilion is one of Mousetail's fishing piers and a fine swim beach. Several families were enjoying the summer weather playing in the water and sunning on the beach the day we visited. Another of the park's hiking trails, the three miles Scenic Trail loops through the woods and over Sparks Ridge from this area. It can also be accessed from the park office or at a point near the campground. The Scenic Trail is a beautiful green walkway with lush green moss along many parts of the pathway. A brochure, attainable at the park office, identifies different trees along the trail. A large variety of birds can also be seen in the park, as well as white-tailed deer.

Fishing is one of the most popular activities at Mousetail Landing State Park. There is a boat ramp on Spring Creek and anglers can fish from their boats or along any of the banks in the park. The bays and creek mouths in the area are especially popular for fishing. Late March through May are the best months for crappie fishing, summer through

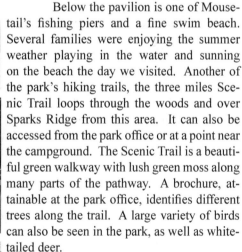

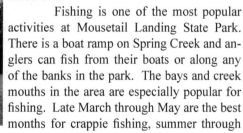

fall for catfish, and spring and fall for bass fishing. Redear sunfish and bluegill can be caught in the river and a number of fishing tournaments are held at the park, including a Junior Fishing Rodeo in summer.

Biking is popular at Mousetail Landing State Park, not only around the grounds but also on the mountain bike trails. The park has one easy four miles long bike trail starting near the pavilion. Another more advanced and difficult nine miles trail travels into the wooded interior of the park, passing Shelters #1 and #2 in a loop route. Horseback riding is also enjoyed in the park with many good riding trails.

A second section of Mousetail Landing is accessed by returning to State Highway #438, turning right, and taking the first right on the other side of Spring Creek embayment out to a point on the Tennessee River. Several short walking trails can be found along the road, with one side road leading to the park's boat launch and another to a fishing pier with picnic tables. The primitive campsite area is located on this road and the loop turnaround point offers fine views across the Tennessee River.

Park rangers at Mousetail Landing offer a number of interpretive and educational programs for visitors, especially in the summer months, such as the Birds of Prey Programs, guided hikes, nature walks, and canoe trips. A Summer Splash Event with a 100-foot slip and slide is held in summer, a Halloween Hay Ride in fall, and a big Easter Egg Hunt in spring. This is a beautiful park with many fine activities to enjoy year round.

David Crockett State Park

Middle Tennessee - Lawrence County
Park Address:1400 West Gaines, Lawrenceburg, TN 38464
Park Size: 1,100 acres   Month Visited: June
Directions: Coming east or west on I-40 toward Nashville, take
the 840 Loop and turn south on I-65. At exit #46 turn east on Hwy
412 to Columbia and travel south on Hwy 43 to Lawrenceburg. In
Lawrenceburg turn west on Hwy 64 and follow to park sign.

Park Description:

Tennessee politician, soldier, and frontiersman Davy Crockett (1786-1836) is a familiar name in American history. Two Tennessee State Parks bear his name—the David Crockett Birthplace State Park in Greene County in East Tennessee and the David Crockett State Park in Lawrence County in Middle Tennessee. We visited both and later drove through Rutherford, in Carroll County in West Tennessee, where Crockett moved his family after a severe Tennessee River flood destroyed his businesses in Lawrence County. Crockett endured unbelievable hardships over his lifetime but overcame them with incredible courage and determination, except the surprise attack by the Mexican Army at the Alamo, where he died at only 49 years of age.

The David Crockett State Park, established in 1959, pays tribute to Crockett's life and to the time he spent living in Lawrence County. He built several successful businesses and served as county justice of the peace and later in the Tennessee General Assembly. Crockett, who was a natural leader, served in many political offices, including The Tennessee Militia as lieutenant colonel and in the U.S. Congress in the House of Representatives from 1827-1831. He grew up on the frontier, one of nine children, and later married Mary Finely and started a family in East Tennessee. After Mary died, Crockett married Elizabeth Patton and moved his family to Lawrence County. The visitor center, as well as the park's museum, provide information about Crockett's life and the powder mill, gristmill, and distillery he built along Shoal Creek in what is now park property. In the town square in nearby Lawrenceburg is another museum and a fine statue of Davy Crockett. Crockett's life was immortalized, and probably overly-glorified, via books about his life, including his 1834 autobiography *A Narrative of the Life of David Crockett*. The 1950s popular television series and song "The

Ballad of Davy Crockett" made Crockett an even more popular folklore legend as "King of the Wild Frontier."

Maps, brochures, and general information about the David Crockett State Park and its trails can also be attained at the visitor center. Behind the center is a large pavilion, popular for events, a picnic area, playground, and tennis courts. A connector trail from the picnic area leads to the beginning of the 1.6 miles Overlook Trail, one of several excellent well-marked trails in this park.

Continuing on the main road beyond the visitor center leads to the first of two campgrounds with a bathhouse, dump station, 54 campsites and eight primitive sites along scenic shaded roads. This camp-

ground is open April 15th through November 15th, while Campground #2 further up the road is open year round. There is also a scout camp area between the two campgrounds with sites for 30 tents.

Past the entrance to Campground #1 on the left is a clear marker for the beginning of the Trail Of Tears National Historic Trail. The marker explains the history of the actual 2.5 miles trail segment used by the Cherokee on their way to Oklahoma. David Crockett, a U.S. Congressman in1830, opposed Jackson's In-

dian Removal Act and was the only Tennessee legislator to vote against it. Historians credit it for the reason Crockett was not reelected for a third Congressional term.

Several inviting pavilions and picnic areas sit alongside the ongoing road, with the Overlook Trail crossing the road to wander behind several picnic sites. The larger Campground #2 nearby has 107 campsites around a series of loop roads with a playground, shelter, dump station, and two bathhouses. Shortly beyond this campground, the main road splits to the right, weaving through the woods to a parking area and a 0.2-mile side trail to Crockett Falls on Shoal Creek. On the hot summer day we visited the park, we found many families wading and playing in the creek below the falls. Another of the park's hiking trails, the Shoal Creek Trail, leads from the falls for 1.7 miles along the creek and through the woods back to Campground #1. Near the parking area for Crockett Falls is a beautiful old covered bridge over the creek, a scenic spot in the park grounds.

On the back of the park loop road is the Crockett Museum and Bird Aviaries. The museum is filled with information and artifacts related to Davy Crockett's life, with a cabin replica scene and a replication of Crockett's gristmill outside. The aviary behind the museum houses local birds, hawks, and owls. Many birds and wildlife, such as wild turkey, deer, and geese, are often spotted around the park, at the lake, or on the hiking trails. Behind the museum is an access point to the park's paved

2.88 miles bike trail, enjoyed by tourists and locals. The trail loops by the park's outdoor amphitheater and ends further up the road behind the park's Olympic swimming pool and recreation area.

A short distance from the museum and pool is Crockett's Mill Restaurant, famous for its home-style buffet and menu items. Flower lined walkways lead to the restaurant and visitors can eat indoors or on an outside patio. Behind the restaurant spreads the beautiful 40-acre Lindsey Lake, a favorite recreational point in the park. Fishing is popular on the lake and visitors can rent rowboats and other watercraft at the boat dock. Canada geese, mallards, herons, and a variety of water birds are often seen on the lake and anglers enjoy fishing off the pier and lakesides. Near the boat dock are seven modern two bedroom, two bath cabins, each with a full kitchen, fireplace, and covered patio. The 0.25 mile Crockett Cabins Trail travels along the lake, and the cabins are all within easy walking distance of the restaurant, pool, and bike trail. David Crockett Park is a beautiful park to visit, well maintained and beloved by both tourists and locals..

A side note: On entering the park via Lawrenceburg we passed many Amish buggies clopping along the main highway and at the entrance to the park was an Amish vegetable stand. Nearby Lawrenceburg is home to the country's oldest Amish Farm. Approximately one hundred families live in the area and while visiting Davy Crockett Park you can visit the Amish Heritage Welcome Center and Country Mall. At the Welcome Center visitors can take a horse drawn buggy ride tour through the Amish community or buy fresh bread, vegetables, quilts, and other authentic Amish products.

Paris Landing

WEST TENNESSEE STATE PARK INDEX

WEST TENNESSEE PARKS

Natchez Trace

Reelfoot Lake

Pickwick Landing

Nathan Bedford Forrest

Nathan Bedford Forrest State Park

West Tennessee - Benton County
Park Address:1825 Pilot Knob Road, Eva, TN 38333
Park Size: 2,587 acres   Month Visited: June
Directions: From I-40, take Hwy 641 north to Camden. Turn
on Hwy 70W Main Street at Camden, following the park signs
through town, turning left on Forrest Avenue and then right on
Hwy 91 through Eva and on to the state park.

Park Description:

   Nathan Bedford Forrest State Park, established in 1963, spreads along
the western shore of the Kentucky Lake impoundment of the Tennessee River, 80
miles upstream from the Kentucky Dam and not far from the small town of Eva.
The state park, first a local park constructed by the Works Progress Administration (WPA) in the Depression era, is named for Nathan Bedford Forrest (1821-
1877), a lieutenant general in the Confederate Army in the Civil War. He was one
of the Civil War's most brilliant tacticians and he played pivotal roles in several
important battles.
   Forrest owned cotton plantations and a trading business in West Tennessee and was an extremely wealthy man when the Civil War started. His ethics
in many areas are questionable but he exemplified great energy and courage.
The state park site was once a strategic military point for the Union Army and

Forrest's Calvary unit launched its 1864 attack on the Johnsonville supply and depot across the Tennessee River from this point. Many statues and memorials have been dedicated to Nathan Bedford Forrest in the South for his military leadership, and in 1929 a memorial to Forrest was erected on Pilot Knob, now included in the state park property.

Our visit began at the visitor center just inside the entrance. The center has a small museum and gift shop and offers maps and information about the park. Behind the center is the 0.3 mile Polk Creek Wildflower Trail, noted as a project of the nearby Camden Garden Club. Along the pathway are many species of wildflowers, offering a pretty walk leading to a lake view and back in a loop. Birds as well as wildflowers are prevalent in the park, with over 100 species noted. Near the Wildflower Trail is a campground area where scouts or other groups can camp by reservation.

Beyond the visitor center, at an intersection of several roads, we followed Happy Hollow Road to the left to another group lodge, to the Happy Hollow RV Campground, and to a ball field, playground, picnic area, and pavilions. The modern group lodge with a big meeting room and kitchen can be rented for events by reservation. The RV campground, the largest in the park, has 37 sites on a quiet loop road with a central bathhouse and dump station. One of the park's hiking trails winds out from the campground and not far down the road is the 0.9 mile Pafford-Wilson Trail.

More than 25 miles of trails can be found in the Nathan Bedford Forrest State Park from short, easy trails to more difficult, rugged ones. Not all the trails in the park are named and the signs at the beginning of most trails do not give you the exact name or expected mileage. We suggest getting a trails map from the visitors

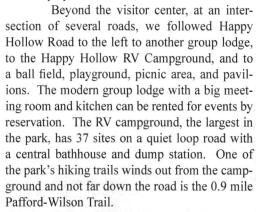

Nathan Bedford Forrest State Park:

* Visitor Center * Museum * Gift Shop * Group Lodge * Playgrounds
* Camping/RV * Picnic * Boating * Fishing * Cabins * Hiking Trails
* Folklife Center * Pavilions

center to help you locate the many trails available.

Nathan Bedford also offers backcountry trails for more serious hikers, some accessible within the main grounds and others from side roads off Harmon Creek Road north of the developed section of the park. These longer trails wander through the forest and by the lakeside, with two backcountry shelters available. Some more remote trails need permits to hike, so check with the visitor center before setting out to explore these backcountry pathways.

Off Happy Hollow Road closer to the park entrance, a left turn leads up to Pilot Knob, passing two more picnic areas and another nice playground, to reach the Tennessee River Interpretive Folklife Center. The center sits high on Pilot Knob with picturesque porches, rocking chairs, benches, and a patio offering stunning views across the Kentucky Lake. The statue to Nathan Bedford Forrest's memory stands prominently on the center's grounds. Inside the center are wildlife and history exhibits with videos in the meeting room on Civil War history, park, and river life. The center also has a gift shop, and behind the center is the beginning of the three miles Nathan Bedford Forrest Trail.

After leaving the Folklife Center, watch for a turn on the right leading to the park's Rustic Log Cabin. This renovated 1930s cabin can actually be rented for overnights or longer stays. Below the cabin is another access point to the Nathan Bedford Forest Trail, which links from the cabin to the Folklife Center on a loop walk through the forest and along the lake.

Near the main entry again, the Lake Front Road leads to the park cabins, boat ramps, more picnic areas, and the Lake Front Campground. On Fossil Point,

seven fine cabins sit along the lake with beautiful views out over the water from their back decks and windows. All have two bedrooms, two baths, full kitchens, fireplaces, and nice amenities on a quiet side road. Further down the Lake Front Road leads to Boat Ramp #1 and a nice swim beach area. We watched several boats launch at this ramp, with most anglers heading out for a happy day on the lake. Fishing is good on the Kentucky Lake from a boat or from the bank. Small creek mouths and embayments along the lake are very popular spots, especially for spring crappie fishing. Smallmouth, largemouth, and striped bass, catfish, sauger, bream, bluegill, and redear sunfish are all caught around the lake. In the summer there is a Fishing Rodeo and free fishing days.

At the end of the Lake Front Road is the park's second boat ramp, a public restroom, picnic area, and the Lake Front Campground. A nice hiking trail wanders along the lakeside for a picturesque stroll with water and woods views. At the Lake Front Campground are 13 sites, most wooden platforms by the lake, with grills and picnic tables, all pretty spots for tents and simple pop-up campers. The views across the lake from this area were gorgeous and we saw kids paddling in the water and enjoying a fine summer day at the lake.

Both Camden and Eva are not far from Nathan Bedford for town visits, and nearby Eva has a city park with a large, sandy swim beach open to the public. Rangers and staff offer many events throughout the year, especially in the summer months. These include hikes, wagon rides, canoe/kayak floats, nature walks, presentations, a Folklife Festival, and a living history weekend. Annual events also include a storytelling event, astronomy day, haunted trail event at Halloween, and an egg hunt at Easter.

Paris Landing State Park

West Tennessee - Henry County
Park Address:16055 Hwy 79N, Buchanan, TN 38222
Park Size: 845 acres   Month Visited: June
Directions: From I-40, take Hwy 641 north to Paris. Turn on Hwy 79 northeast at park signs and follow to the park entrance.

Park Description:

 Paris Landing State Park lies on the widest part of the Kentucky Lake on the Tennessee River not far from the Kentucky border and Land Between the Lakes National Recreation Area. We found it to be one of the most beautiful state parks on the water in the state. The park is definitely a boating, fishing, waterskiing, and swimming paradise, not to mention a beautiful place to play golf.

 After entering the park boundary, look for the visitor center as the highway nears the long, arched Ned Ray McWherter Bridge over the river. The recently remodeled visitor center is a great place to pick up maps and information about the 845 acres park. Near the visitor center is the blue-roofed Paris Landing State Park Marina. Scenic ramps walk down to the marina that sits on the lake with a network of ramps and walkways leading out in all directions to piers filled with boats of all types and shapes, ready for a day on the water. We loved walking down the long wooden walkways to see the boats and to enjoy the views of the gorgeous expanse of the Kentucky Lake. The full-service marina sells gas, ice, drinks, bait, fishing licenses, and general supplies, has a transportation ser-

vice to points around the park, and it offers covered and open boat slips for monthly or yearly rental fees. Near the marina are a day-use courtesy dock, public boat launch area, restrooms, and a fish cleaning station.

A side road to the right of the marina swings around to a picnic area on a peninsula of land reaching into the lake with beautiful views. A truss section of the original Scott Fitzhugh Bridge, built and first installed in 1937, is located on this peninsula point, a reminder of the narrow bridge once used to cross the Tennessee River. Behind the picnic area is a big fishing pier on the water. The pier is a favorite spot for individual or family fishing and the pier stretches in several directions to offer room for all.

Returning to the marina, a side road winds behind the visitor center to the park's campground. The shady campsite has 45 sites that can accommodate RVs up to 38 feet, 18 primitive campsites, picnic tables, grills, a park laundry, and two bathhouses. For campers and visitors to the north side of the park, an overpass road leads directly over the busy highway to the other side of the state park.

Across the highway is the championship golf course. The Paris Landing State Park Golf Course is a tree-lined par-72, 18-hole course with a nice balance of rolling land, trees and water, with several holes skirting the Kentucky Lake.

Paris Landing State Park:
* Visitor Center * Marina * Boating * Camping/RV * Fishing * Hiking
* Paris Landing State Park Golf Course * Hiking Trails * Cabins
* Conference Center * Swimming Pool * Inn * Restaurant * Tennis
* Basketball * Volleyball * Boat Launch Ramps * Ball fields

Along the lake golfers can spot bald eagle nests high on telephone poles, the poles erected for them in the water, and feeders around the course encourage birds, wild turkeys, and other animals. The course received a Certified Audubon Cooperative Sanctuary designation from Audubon for maintaining a high degree of environmental quality and was awarded a 4-Star Award by Golf Digest every year since 1995. Amenities include a driving range, practice green, pull carts, clubhouse, and snack bar.

Continuing past the golf course leads to Paris Landing's hiking trails and rental cabins. The park has 10 modern, spacious three-bedroom, two bath cabins facing the lake. Each has a wide deck with scenic views across the water, picnic tables, and full amenities.

Several of the hiking trails begin near the cabins. Three main trails are listed for the park, the three miles long Red Tail Loop, the shorter 0.6 mile White Tail Loop, and a one mile Healthy Hike Trail. Many walking trails lattice around the area grounds, and walking and biking on the quiet streets through the park are popular with visitors. Trails are well-maintained and in spring a variety of wildflowers can be seen along the trailsides.

The road winding from the cabins and golf course over to the eastern part of the park passes the conference center and the Olympic-sized public swimming pool with a big children's wading pool and snack bar. A second guest pool can be found behind the Paris Landing Inn overlooking the beautiful Kentucky Lake.

We spent the night at the inn in one of its 130 guestrooms, all with balconies providing breathtaking views across the Kentucky Lake. The Riverboat Restaurant inside the inn offers excellent breakfast, lunch, and dinner buffets along with menu selections, and the restaurant's wide windows provide scenic views of the lake while you enjoy your meal.

Also at the far eastern end of the park is another picnic area and large pavilion on the waterfront with a sandy public swim beach. Visitors will also find an open air theater, playground, basketball and tennis courts, baseball diamond, white sand volleyball court, and quiet walkways along the lake. Fishing is enjoyed from the bank as well as from boats out in the lake. A wide variety of fish can be caught on the banks of the 106,000 acres Kentucky Lake or in the little bays along the shorelines. Catfish, crappie, bluegill, and bass are common catches. In addition, a number of fishing tournaments, derbies, and kids' fishing rodeos are held on the lake.

This park is an active place in all seasons, especially in the warmer months. Rangers and employees host a variety of events including kayak and canoe tours, swim lessons and water aerobics at the pool, a 4th of July fireworks display, boating programs, craft activities, and free concerts, to name only a few. On the hiking trails and in quiet spots along the lakeside you may see turkey, fox, and coyote as well as white-tailed deer and a wide variety of songbirds and water birds. Don't miss stopping by this park on any visit to the Land Between the Lakes area.

163

Big Cypress Tree State Park

West Tennessee - Weakley County
Park Address:295 Big Cypress Rd, Greenfield, TN 38230
Park Size: 27 acres   Month Visited: June
Directions: From I-40 at Jackson, take Hwy 45E north to Green-
field. Past Greenfield, turn west on Hwy 445 Kimery Store Road
and follow approximately 8 miles to park entrance on the right.

Park Description:

Big Cypress Tree State Park holds the title for the smallest state park in Tennessee at only 27 acres. Located in rural Weakley County, it sits adjacent to the larger Big Cypress State Recreational Natural Area. The entire tract lies in the forested bottomlands and flood plain of the Obion and Middle Fork Obion rivers.

The park is named for the giant cypress tree that once stood in the bottomlands of this area. Referred to as "The Tennessee Titan" the tree stood at 175 feet tall, 40 feet in circumference, 13 feet in diameter, and was estimated to be 1,350 years old. The big cypress was the largest bald cypress in the United States and the largest tree of any species east of the Mississippi River. Unfortunately in 1976, lightning struck the old cypress causing it to die. With the tree gone, the old trail to view the giant cypress is now closed and the site of the tree cannot be seen when visiting the park.

Big Cypress Tree State Park, small and a little out of the way for travelers, is beloved by locals in the area. It is a clean, peaceful, well-kept park with a nice play area, covered pavilion, picnic tables, ball field, playground, and a walking nature trail. The paved nature trail winds in a 0.38 mile loop around the picnic area and provides an easy walk for all. A kiosk tells about the area and about native trees and flowers visitors might see.

Along the trail is a Wildflower Garden with coneflowers, black-eyed Susans, primrose, and other native wildflowers. Trees are identi-

164

fied with markers along the trail-side and the pathway is ADA accessible, also fine for strollers or bikes. Big Cypress has restroom facilities but no visitor center. Visitors can get needed information about the park from the ranger at his residence and designated park office down the road on the left beyond the picnic and play area.

Beyond the ranger's house, the road leads to a 1,142-foot long wooden boardwalk leading through the cypress bottomland. The trail begins on a paved walkway winding by an old barn and around to the start of the boardwalk. The new boardwalk, opened in 2015, passes through a bottomland and semi-flooded forest around sloughs and pools. The trail leads to several overlooks over the swampy area and visitors will spot old cypress trees along the route as well as other native trees and plants. Signs identify many tree species and the park has plans to extend the boardwalk in the future to reach the Middle Fork Obion River. A rough River Trail still leads to the river but is not open to the public. Mosquitoes should be anticipated in this bottomland forest area, so bring bug spray repellent.

Big Cypress Tree Park hosts a Fall Festival in early November, interpretive walks, scout camporees, and many local events. A kiosk in the park tells visitors about the nearby David Crockett cabin and museum in Rutherford, approximately 10 miles from the park, a pleasant side trip for visitors to the area. Crockett hunted and fished extensively in the park and Big Cypress region while he lived in West Tennessee.

Natchez Trace State Park

West Tennessee - Henderson County
Park Address: 24845 Natchez Trace Rd, Wildersville, TN 38388
Park Size: 1,095 acres   Month Visited: June
Directions: From I-40, take exit 116 south on Hwy 114 into park's
main entrance on Natchez Trace Road.

Park Description:

Natchez Trace State Park is located approximately halfway between Nashville and Jackson, Tennessee. The parkland lies within the 48,000 acres state forest and wildlife management area sprawling across Henderson, Carroll, and Benton Counties on either side of Interstate 40. The 1,095 acres state park, south of I-40, is broken into three main sections. After passing one of the early hiking trails and picnic spots on the left, watch for the park office and visitor center on the right.

The center has a gift shop, bird aviary, maps and information, and a museum explaining the history of the park. The Natchez Trace acreage, which gradually became heavily eroded, overly timbered, and unusable for farming, was reclaimed by the government in the 1930s New Deal reclamation programs. In the center, remember to look at the old photos from the 1930s to see the amazing job the park has done to restore the land. We also enjoyed observing the birds in the center aviary and watching a park ranger working with a group of Junior Rangers. Be sure to get a map to find your way in this large park.

A short distance from the visitor center lies the Equestrian Center and the road to the Bucksnort Wrangler Campground with 62 sites, a bathhouse, dump station, hitching rails, and playground. Natchez Trace is a great location for horseback riding with 250 miles of trails. The park is also latticed with hiking trails from short ones, like the one mile Fair View Gullies loop, to longer trails like the 40-miles long Red Leaves Trail. Twenty-three miles of trails wind along the park's lakesides and forest pathways, and a map of the more popular hiking trails, horse trails, and the 50 miles of mountain bike trails can be attained at the visitor center

Beyond the Equestrian Center near the general store is the Five Point Group Lodge. Nearby are rental cottages, a nice picnic area, a large playground, the old fire tower, and a big softball field. A kids' tournament group, staying in the park, were practicing on the field the day we visited. Following the signs beyond the fire tower leads to a road to the 167 acres Browns Creek Lake.

A favorite spot for fishing, the lake has a fishing pier, boat ramp, and jon boats which are available on a first come basis for visitors who want to fish on the lake or simply enjoy a boat ride.

Continuing around from the Browns Lake area leads to another scenic lake, the 690 acres Pin Oak Lake with even more accessible points for visitor fun. Pin Oak Lake has nice cabins and villas along the lakeside, boat docks, ramps, pavilions and picnic areas. On a beautiful peninsula by the lake is the Pin Oak RV Campground, one of five camping areas. The campground can accommodate any size RV, with 77-sites, two bathhouses, a big pavilion, playground, swim beach, and archery range. Pin Oak

Lake, the park's largest lake, allows motorboats, pontoon boats, wave runners, and ski boats, and on the warm June day we visited we spotted many visitors enjoying skiing and boating fun on the water. Several pavilions and picnic areas can be found around the lake and one of our favorites was Pin Oak Shelter #1 on the lake near the Scout Camp. This is a quiet secluded spot with beautiful vistas over the water and access to the 1.05 miles long Pin Oak Trail.

Another side road, the Pin Oak Lodge Road, leads to the 47-room Pin Oak Lodge situated on a hillside overlooking the lake. All the rooms have lovely views across the water or of the big swimming pool, patio, and play area behind the lodge. Excellent meeting room space for group events can be rented at the inn, including three conference rooms and the Natchez Room with over 1,000 square feet of banquet space. Outdoor patios, benches along the lake, and quiet walking trails make this a perfect spot for guests and events. Cabin and inn guests can also rent canoes or kayaks at the inn.

We spent the night in the lodge and also enjoyed the lodge's Western Spur Restaurant that offers breakfast, lunch, and dinner menu items and a seasonal buffet. The buffet is available when the inn is busy but meals off the menu are always available. When the breakfast buffet isn't offered the inn provides a free continental breakfast, nicer than in most hotels.

Parsons Road, by the small store, leads to Natchez Trace's third main area, situated around the 58 acres Cub Lake. Our favorite thing about this park was exploring around the different lakes—all beautiful. On a side road on Cub Lake is the Recreation Lodge, another excellent spot for group events. The historic building was constructed by the Civilian Conservation Corps in the 1930s and is a pretty facility with plenty of parking.

Access to the popular 4 miles Cub Lake Trail can be found near the lodge as well as the beginning of the half-mile Fern Self-Guided Nature Trail loop. A highlight on Cub Lake is the long rustic footbridge leading across an arm of the

lake to the public beach and day use area. It allows access from the cabins and campground to a fine sand swim beach and boat rental facility.

Seventeen pretty cabins sit along the lakeside and both the camping areas are nice ones. Cub Lake Campground #1, with 23 sites, and Campground #2, with 46 sites, have bathhouses and waste stations, and both are able to host small RVs, pop ups, and tent campers. None are far from the beach and boat rental facility. Paddleboats, jon boats, and canoes can be rented by the hour and the Cub Lake Swimming Beach is one of the largest we've seen at any state park. Fishermen and women often fish off the long footbridge and along the banks of Cub Lake and other lakes in the park. Bass, catfish, and bluegill are prevalent and fishing licenses can be purchased at the Pin Oak Inn.

Many families come year after year to this big state park for vacation weeks and fun weekends with so many lake and recreational facilities to choose from. With a park of this size, planned programs are available year-round such as hikes, hayrides, birds of prey demonstrations, wildlife programs, and Junior Ranger Day Camps. Visitors can also enjoy the Fall Festival, Heritage Day, an Easter Egg hunt in spring, ranger-led outdoor classrooms, trail runs, guided horseback rides, an Annual Kids Fishing Rodeo, Turkey Shoots, a Kayak Fishing Tournament, and more. There is always something fun going on at Natchez Trace State Park.

169

Pinson Mounds State Park

West Tennessee - Madison County
Park Address: 460 Ozier Road, Pinson, TN 38366
Park Size: 1,300 acres   Month Visited: June
Directions: From I-40 at Jackson, take US Hwy 45S to the town of
Pinson. Turn left at the park sign onto State Hwy 197 and follow
the signs 2.3 miles to the park entrance.

Park Description:

        Pinson Mounds State Park and Archaeological Area is an interesting
park to visit and explore and would be of special interest to those fascinated by
archeology. The entire archeological complex of the park spreads over 400 acres
and includes about 17 earthen mounds dating back to the Middle Woodland period from 200 B.C. to 500 A. D. Pinson is the largest Middle Woodland earthwork
center in the southeastern United States and is designated a Registered National
Historic Landmark. The mounds incorporate astronomical alignments in their architecture with a blend of architectural styles, and evidence suggests the mounds
served both burial and ceremonial purposes.

        The park has two pavilions, a playground
and group camp area but no other traditional park
amenities. The entry road to the camp winds from
the highway around in a loop road to the main
parking lot in front of the visitor center, office,
and Interpretive Center Museum all housed in one
large building that looks like a Native American
Indian Mound. Inside the museum's 4,500 square
feet of exhibit space are artifact exhibits, interpretive panels, an 80-seat theater and Discovery
Room for historical exploration. The park office,
an archaeological library, and the West Tennessee
Regional Archaeology Office all make their home
in the building. There's a dugout canoe in the museum, skulls of old animals, pots and urns, imple-

ments, arrowheads, early weapons, drawings and more.

Immediately behind the museum is the park's largest mound Saul's Mound. At 72 feet with a base of 370 feet by 300 feet, it is the central mound in the Pinson Complex. Its four corners point to the cardinal directions of north, south, east and west, and one hypothesis suggests the top of the mound was the observation point for

observing the Equinox sunrises and Summer Solstice. Once covered in trees and ground cover, the state recently had to remove all the trees from Saul's Mound as they were threatening the mound's structure. A 90 foot wooden stairway winds up the back of Saul's Mound to a high, railed observation deck offering a panoramic view of the entire area.

Two other mounds, more like small rolling hillocks, lie in the vicinity of Saul's Mound. Other trails and walkways network east and west from Saul's Mound to all the other mounds and earthen works in the park. A broad paved trail leads south through the back of the park, passing by the Central Mound Group and Barrow Pit. Beyond the pit, a side path angles right to the Duck's Nest Access mound. Back out on the main trail, a boardwalk passes through a cypress swamp to an overlook on the South Fork Forked Deer River.

A Nature Trail from the boardwalk winds around behind the Earthworks to the Outer and Inner Loop Trails and by Mounds 28, 29, and 30. Many of the mounds blend into the landscape like hills, but signs along the trails explain each mound and its significance. To the west side of the park the Hudson Bay Trail leads for about a mile across the Hudson Branch to reach the Western Mound Group, Ozier Mound 5, Mound 31, and the Twin Mounds—the latter of which were burial mounds. Plan on doing some walking to explore the entire park and bring bug repellent.

Chickasaw State Park

West Tennessee - Chester and Hardeman Counties
Park Address: 20 Cabin Lane, Henderson, TN 38340
Park Size: 1,400 acres   Month Visited: June
Directions: From I-40 at Jackson, take US Hwy 45S to Henderson
and turn west on Hwy 100 to park entrance.

Park Description:

Chickasaw State Park lies approximately 30 minutes and 18 miles south of Jackson, Tennessee, outside of Henderson. It's a lovely park, with the main public portion spread around Lake Placid. Further west, eight miles from the main park, a group camp sits on Lake LaJoie, a second smaller lake, but this area of the park is only open to the public when the Group Camp is vacant. The entire area lies within 14,384 acres of timberland and forest, mostly managed by the State Forestry Division and the Tennessee Wildlife Resources Agency. Named

for the Chickasaw Indians who once hunted and made their homes in this area, Chickasaw officially became a state park in 1955.

A visitor center and office sits on a hill on the left beyond the main entry sign with a pretty fishpond in front. Maps and information can be picked up inside including a list of on-going events and activities. Beyond the visitor center, Cabin Road leads directly to the 54 acre Placid Lake. Beside the lake is a large, pictur-esque recreation area including a pavilion and picnic tables, playground, swim beach, bath-house, group lodge, and boat dock. This is the hub of Chickasaw State Park and a popular spot where families enjoy spending the day. Above the lake area on a hillside is the old Sagamore Lodge, a historic stone and brick building constructed in the 1930s. The lodge, with its rock fireplace and rustic architecture, is a favorite venue for events, parties, group gatherings, square dancing, reunions, dinners, and meetings.

Across the street from the lodge is a large parking area, with picnic tables and pavilions nestled on the hills around it. One of the park's hiking trails, the 0.65 mile Forked Pine Trail weaves out of the back of the parking area and later links to the 1.15 miles Friend's Trail for a longer hike. There are several other pleasant trails in the main park area including a 1.5 miles long Lakeshore Trail looping around the lake's edge and the Fern Creek Trail beginning at the main campground. Bikes are allowed on all roadways and there are many miles of additional mountain bike roads in the adjacent Chickasaw Forest.

A trail winds down from Sycamore Lodge to the covered boat dock and rental boat facility. We saw many visitors enjoying pedal boats on the lake the day we visited. Canoes, jon boats, kayaks, and pedal boats can be rented at the boat dock in summer and jon boats can be rented at the park office year-round. Visitors can also bring their own kayaks and canoes to the lake to enjoy. Boating and fishing are popular on the lake year round, with catfish, bass, bream, and other fish caught. When the group camp is vacant visitors can also boat and fish on Lake LaJoie.

The Lake LaJoie Group Camp is an excellent place for a group gathering. It is private, sitting separate from the main park area on its own private lake, and has a big lodge with a dining hall, 17 historic cabins, men's and women's bathrooms, picnic areas, and pavilions. Swimming and boating can be enjoyed on the lake and the scenic 1.8-miles Lake Lajoie Trail winds around the lakeside. Reservations to use the camp can be made at the park office.

The Group Lodge on Lake Placid, as well as the Sycamore Lodge, are also fine spots for group meetings and events. The Group Lodge, in addition to its meeting area and kitchen, has bunkrooms for overnights. In an ideal

Chickasaw State Park:

* Visitor Center * Picnic Areas * Playgrounds * Swimming * Boating
* Group Lodge * Hiking Trails * Cabins * Camping/RV Sites * Tennis
* Restaurant * Ball Fields * Horse Stable * Chickasaw Golf Course

location, both lodges are within walking distance of the lake's swim beach, pavilion, picnic area, and boat dock.

The main swim beach is a big, flat sandy area alongside Lake Placid with a retaining wall and steps leading down into the water. The swim area is roped off with the water shallow enough for children to enjoy. Around the beach are shady picnic spots, benches, and a playground. Canada geese and mallards love the waterfront here and visitors will see many of them, on and around the lakeside, and can observe other birds throughout the park. A flyer from the visitor's center details more than 100 species of birds recorded in the area.

A wooden boardwalk crosses the lake not far from the swim beach, and across the road from the boardwalk are the rental cabins. There are 13 cute historic cabins, many with lake views. Each have nice decks, grills, and picnic tables for outdoor enjoyment along with full kitchens and baths inside. A walk across the boardwalk over the lake leads to a tent campground with 29 sites. Further west in the park is a large RV campground with 52 sites, a bathhouse, dump station, playground, and amphitheater. Both camping areas have picnic tables and grills and are on quiet shady streets in the park.

The Chickasaw State Park Restaurant sits on Lake Levee Road behind Lake Placid across from the boat dock and only a short walk from the lodges and swim beach. It serves southern meals and offers seasonal buffets. Management changes were going on at the restaurant when we visited, as were some improvements and repairs in the park's campgrounds and to the boardwalk across the lake.

All parks, like other properties, have updates in progress now and then, so expect to see some nice improvements at Chickasaw by the time this book publishes.

Near the restaurant, a side road leads to the historic Brewer's Cabin. The old cabin was originally built in 1876 and donated to the park by Max and Ruby Nell Brewer to show park visitors how settlers in the 1800s lived. There are sheds and an outhouse beside the cabin and an access point to the 1.5 miles Fern Creek Trail. Not far down the road from the cabin on Campground Road are the big ball field, tennis courts, a multi-purpose sports field, picnic area, pavilion, big RV campground, and a riding stable.

The stable offers horseback rides on five miles of trails or visitors can bring their own horses and rent stalls at the stables. Hundreds of miles of trails wander through the Chickasaw State Forest for riders to enjoy and the park offers a Wrangler Campground near the stables, too. It has 32 sites, a nearby riding arena, and access to a one hour trail ride leading across Piney Creek and into the state forest. The stable is privately leased, so check with the stable directly for hours and fees.

After leaving the stable and passing the campground, camp store, and amphitheater, the main road meets Highway 100 again. Continuing west on the highway leads to the Bear Trace and Chickasaw Golf Course and the Lake LaJoie Group Camp area. The golf course, opened in 2014. has a fine clubhouse and snack bar and offers a beautiful 18-hole, Jack Nicklaus' designed 7,118 yards layout and driving range. The course is managed by David Chasteen.

Pickwick Landing State Park

West Tennessee - Hardin County
Park Address: 116 State Park Lane, Counce, TN 38326
Park Size: 1,533 acres   Month Visited: June
Directions: From I-40 at Jackson, take US Hwy 45 South toward
Henderson. Continue through Selmer and turn east on Hwy 57 to
Counce and follow the park signs into the park. From east Ten-
nessee, take exit 143 to Hwy 13 south. Follow through Lobelville
and Linden, swinging southeast on Hwy 128 beyond Clifton and
west on Hwy 64 toward Savannah. At park sign, take bypass 226
around Savannah, leading to 128 south, across the dam, and to
Hwy 57 to the park entrance.

Park Description:

Pickwick Landing was once a riverboat landing on the Tennessee River.
The area's first postmaster, a fan of Charles Dickens, named his post office Pickwick in honor of Dickens' novel *Pickwick Papers*. In the 1930s as a part of Roosevelt's New Deal projects Pickwick Dam was built, creating the 43,100 acres
and 53 miles long Pickwick Lake. The construction of the dam and resulting
floodwaters displaced over 506 families in the area and partially submerged parts
of two small towns. The old Pickwick White Sulphur Cemetery in the middle of
the park serves as a reminder of the thriving community once in this area. Much
of the parkland was once home to the TVA construction crews and their families
working to build the Pickwick Dam. After the dam was completed the government sent Civilian Conservation Corps workers in 1935 to begin building the

recreation area that is now the park. TVA governed the park's lands until the state of Tennessee began acquiring the land and created Pickwick Landing State Park in 1970.

The 1,533 acres park has a stunning marina, modern inn and restaurant, cabins, campground, golf course, three public swimming beaches, boat launches, and multiple picnic and recreational sites. It is a popular place in all seasons. Our exploration started at the visitor center and office where we talked with park rangers for ideas about things to do and see and picked up brochures and a map. Beyond the visitor center we looped left off the main Park Road to find The Inn at Pickwick Landing, set in a beautiful location on the lake with multi-colored crepe myrtles in full bloom in a small garden area beside the front entry. The inn has 119 rooms, each with lovely views of the lake. The inn also has both an outdoor and indoor pool, spacious meeting rooms, a gift shop, exercise room, and a gracious lobby centered around a rock fireplace. Inside the inn is the Captain's Galley Restaurant, serving fine Southern cuisine for breakfast, lunch, and dinner in a spacious dining room with scenic lake views.

Behind the inn is a paved 1.2 miles walking trail that winds along the lakeside, leading to the nearby picnic area and a courtesy boat dock. Benches, swings and picnic tables dot the shore, offering spots looking out over Pickwick Lake. Continuing past the inn is a picnic area on a peninsula of the lake and two of the park's sandy swim beaches, Circle Beach and Sandy Beach. The road passes by the old cemetery along the way,

and trails and side roads lead to scenic pavilions and picnic areas on the hillsides by the lake. A nice boat launch, tennis courts, a playground, and a disc golf course can also be enjoyed. Even during the week the park was busy with visitors picnicking along the lakeside, swimming on the beaches, fishing and skiing out on the river, or just relaxing in a lounge chair to look out over the beauty of Pickwick Lake.

Returning to the main road and swinging around an embayment in the lake, brings visitors to the handsome marina, one of the largest we've seen at any state park. The marina rents covered and uncovered slips for boats and sailboats up to 80 feet, monthly or yearly, and offers overnight dockage. The marina store sells general supplies, ice, gas, diesel fuel, and has restrooms, showers, and a laundry. It also has a large boat launch and provides transportation service to the inn, golf course, and campground. Canoes, fishing boats, and pontoon boats can be rented at the marina and picnic tables sit in shady spots around the lake. This is a beautiful facility, and with so much water accessibility, fishing as well as skiing and recreational boating is popular. The park is known for great sport fishing and several local and national fishing tournaments are held here. White and largemouth bass, catfish, striped bass, and sauger are common catches.

Off the Marina Road are the park's 17 rental cabins, ten original and seven newer ones, all with one or two bedrooms, full kitchens, fireplaces, outdoor patios, and picnic tables. Guests staying in the cabins can use the inn's swimming pools and tennis courts. The cabins lie along a scenic finger of the lake and the 2.8

miles long Island Loop Trail begins near the start of the cabin road. This shady hiking trail winds back through the woods, linking in several loops, to the campground area and out to a point on the Pickwick Lake.

Off Hardin Dock Road not far from the cabin area is Pickwick Landing's large wooded campground with 48 sites. The campground, open year-round, has a check-in station, bathhouse, and dump station, with sites for all type of campers. Across the lake, the Burton Branch Recreational Area has 33 more sites, good for tent and pop-up campers with a bathhouse, playground, and a boat ramp for easy access to the lake.

Near the park entrance is the golf course, a beautiful and challenging course where many district, local events, and area tournaments are held including the St. Jude's Charity Golf Tournament. Every hole is tree-lined with well-kept fairways and pristine greens and the course is a favorite of local and visiting golfers. The course, designed by Jack Nicklaus and Joe Lee, has a small clubhouse and a driving range with shuttle transportation provided to the inn, marina, and campground.

Many popular events and activities occur year-round at Pickwick Landing State Park including the Bufford Pusser Festival in May, the Fourth of July Fireworks and Catfish World Championship Fishing Tournament in July, Tennessee River Run in September, Christmas in the Park and Holiday Mart in December, along with ranger-led programs. This beautiful state park on Pickwick Lake should be one on your "To See" Bucket List.

Big Hill Pond State Park

West Tennessee - McNairy County
Park Address: 1435 John Howell, Pochahontas, TN 38061
Park Size: 4,138 acres   Month Visited: June
Directions: From I-40 at Jackson, take US Hwy 45S to Henderson. Continue on Hwy 45S through Selmer south and turn west on Hwy 57, follow Hwy 57 through Ramer to park on left just before Pochahontas.

Park Description:

Big Hill Pond is for the individual who wants a rustic, out-of-the way spot to hike or camp. The larger percentage of the park spreads through forested timberland and bottomland between the highway on the north and Cypress Creek and the Tuscumbia River to the south. Much of the area is only accessible by hiking. The developed portion of the park lies near the entrance off the main road that leads to the visitor center. Within Big Hill Pond grounds visitors will find a small playground, picnic area, campground, and a boat dock on the 165 acres Travis McNatt Lake.

The park is named for the 35 acres Big Hill Pond, formed in the 1800s as water filled a borrow pit initially excavated for the building of a levee across the Tuscumbia River and Cypress Creek for the Memphis and Charleston Railroad. This dug out area left a pit deep enough to later fill with water and create the Big Hill Pond near the back of the park property. The pond lies in a swampy, bottomland area now full of cypress trees and it is not accessible by vehicle.

After entering the park, drive down the road to find the main office. If the office is open you can get information, register to camp, pick up a hiking trails map, and get hiking advice from one of the rangers. On the entry road before the office is a playground, pavilion, picnic tables, a group event building on a hillside, and several hiking trails. A big sign leads into the park's horse trail area with a 13 miles riding trail, also shared with mountain bikers. A short distance beyond the office is the small campground area with 28 rustic campsites with tables, grills, and a bathhouse.

180

Travis McNutt Lake is a pretty spot at the end of the main road. It has a boat dock, benches, picnic tables, walking trails along the lakeside, and access to a long wooden boardwalk across an embayment of the lake. Canoes, kayaks, and small boats with electric trolling motors are allowed on the lake and anglers can fish by boat or along the banks.

Big Hill Pond has·30 miles of hiking trails, many crossing and interlinking. This is not a park for casual day hikes so come prepared for backcountry trail hiking with proper clothing, good boots or walking shoes, water, and a good insect repellent. Wildlife is prevalent—deer, ducks, geese, owls, otters, muskrats, a wide variety of birds—and in remote sections there is the possibility of snakes. Four backcountry shelters with bunks are scattered along the trails for overnight stays.

One of the most popular hikes is a one-and-a-half hour hike through Dismal Swamp and across the 0.8-mile boardwalk to a high, metal 70 foot observation tower. A climb to the top gives views out over the park. Other trails weave around Travis McNutt Lake, to Big Hill Pond and deep into the remote end of the park near the Tuscumbia River and Cypress Creek. Rugged and off the beaten path, the park and trails are never crowded.

T.O. Fuller State Park

West Tennessee - Shelby County
Park Address: 1500 West Mitchell Road, Memphis, TN 38109
Park Size: 1,138 acres   Month Visited: June
Directions: From I-40 into Memphis, swing left on I-240 around
the city, exit on Hwy 51 South and then west on Winchester Road.
Follow Winchester into W. Mitchell Road directly into the park.

Park Description:

Located in the southern limits of the city of Memphis, near the Mississippi River and the state's western boundary, T. O. Fuller State Park offers a quiet oasis in the midst of an inner city environment. Begun in 1938 during the Great Depression, the park was built by the Civilian Conservation Corps (CCC) on what was once a vast cotton plantation on the Mississippi River. During construction, the CCC discovered Native American artifacts. This park section was subsequently studied and developed by University of Tennessee archeologists and is now known as Chucalissa, declared a National Historic Landmark in 1994.

At the office and visitor center, maps and brochures about the park and Chucalissa can be attained. Beside the office, the four miles Discovery Trail begins, that loops throughout the park grounds. To the right beyond the office a side road leads to a beautiful recreation area with picnic areas and three pavilions, a fine swimming pool complex with an Olympic-sized pool and wading pool, bath house and concessions area, tennis and basketball courts. Parking is abundant and it is easy to imagine families and groups enjoying this lovely area. The near-

by golf course and clubhouse are now closed, replaced by the T.O. Fuller Interpretive Center and a new series of trails through the former golf course called the Wildlife Enhancement Area. Guided tours, talks, and nature walks are available, conducted by rangers or staff, and the space can be rented for meetings and events.

Boxtown Road off the main road leads to a group camp, pavilion, play area with a large basketball court, and the park's campground. There are 45 campsites, large enough to accommodate RVs, a dump station, and a nice shower and restroom facility with a laundry and an ice machine. The campground is clean and pretty, set on shaded streets, and only ten minutes to downtown Memphis attractions and seven minutes to Graceland.

Beyond the campground, Chucalissa Road leads off Steam Plant Road to the Chucalissa Indian Village and Wetlands. At the end of the road is C.H. Nash Museum. The museum can be toured for a fee and features two exhibit halls with artifacts and interpretive exhibits. There is a hands-on archaeology lab in the museum where visitors can examine prehistoric artifacts up to 10,000 years old. Group educational programs and family days are held by the museum and a museum store offers handcrafted items from Native American artisans, like pottery, jewelry, and books. A nature trail leads back to the Native American Indian mounds constructed between 1000-1500 AD and to a wetlands area where a large Native American community once stood.

This historic site, the first state park to open for African Americans east of the Mississippi River, is named for Dr. Thomas O. Fuller (1867-1942). Fuller was a church and civic leader who spent his life working to educate and empower African Americans. A Fuller Fest is held at the park each October to celebrate the unique history of this state park.

Meeman-Shelby Forest State Park

West Tennessee - Shelby County
Park Address: 910 Riddick Road, Millington, TN 38053
Park Size: 12,539 acres   Month Visited: June
Directions: From I-40 loop above Memphis, exit Hwy 300 West
onto Hwy 51 North toward Millington. In a little over four miles,
turn left onto Hwy 388/North Watkins Street. Follow for about
seven miles until it dead-ends. Turn left onto Locke Cuba Road.
At the four-way stop turn right following park signs, and in about
a mile turn left into the park.

Park Description:

The Meeman-Shelby Forest State Park, about 35 minutes from Memphis, is a vast tract on the Chickasaw Bluffs above the Mississippi River. The park lies between two large Wildlife Management Areas (WMA) and includes Eagle Lake, an expansive swamp. Two-thirds of the Meeeman-Shelby Forest State Park consists of bottomland hardwood forests of large oak, cypress, and tupelo, including a Bald Cypress and Tupelo swamp. Several of the state's largest trees can be found in the park, and the area is often termed an unspoiled forest, with ravines, dense forest areas, swampland, and miles of hiking, biking, and horse trails. The park was named for Edward J. Meeman (1888-1996), editor for the Memphis newspaper and a courageous conservationist, who in the early 1930s helped to convince state officials to purchase Shelby Forest to establish a state park.

Because the area is so vast, it is wise to stop at the visitor center to get a map of the park and helpful information. There is also a small museum at the center, a gift shop, a large topographical map of the grounds under glass, and outside the center a natural area and gazebo. Beyond the center the road swings right through the forest to head to a campground and group

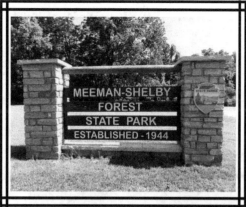

camp. Piersol Group Camp is centered in a wooded area around a rustic lodge that can house up to 140 people by reservation. The camp is tucked away from the road near 32 acres Piersol Lake. The small lake, hidden in the forest and not readily accessible to the public, provides a quiet spot for fishing or canoeing.

At the end of the road to the group camp are access points to two of the park's hiking trails, the Woodland Trail, a 3.5 miles loop, and the five miles long Biking and Hiking Trail. The wide bike trail is mostly paved, moderate on the upper level but steeper further on. Both trails are nice ones for park visitors to take a short or long hike on. The park, as might be expected of such a vast acreage, has over 20 miles of trails, many travel-

ing through rugged, forested pathways, with steep climbs, overgrown areas, and often challenging terrain. Two other well-known trails, besides the Woodland and Biking Trail, are the four miles long Pioneer Springs Trail, beginning near

the Nature Center and the strenuous, steep eight miles Chickasaw Bluff Trail. Most Meeman-Shelby Forest trails are hilly and woodsy. It is wise to wear practical clothes and boots or walking shoes for these back-country hikes, carrying water and insect repellent. Keep in mind that mosquitoes, gnats, and other insects can be expected in bottomland near a major river. Wildlife are prevalent along the trails and in the park, including turkey, deer, geese, hawks, owls, raccoons, beaver, foxes, snakes, and over 240 species of birds.

The next road beyond the group camp road leads to a large camp-ground. The campground has 49 sites, big enough for RVs, with tables and grills, a dump station, and a bathhouse, all situated along a quiet wooded road. Beyond the campground area a one-way road leads over to the historic Civilian Conservation Corps (CCC) Mississippi River Camp, now being restored, and to the start of the Chickasaw Bluff Trail. The road then winds downhill to the Sasser Boat Launch on the Mississippi River, built in the 1930s by the CCC. Boats can be launched from the wide boat ramp or visitors can sit for a while to watch the barges and boats go by on the river.

Back within the main park area, a left turn from the visitor center curls past several more shaded picnic shelters and play areas to a right turn winding down to 125 acres Poplar Tree Lake. Along the way the road passes a large 36-hole disc golf course on the left, the park's swim-ming pool, closed at our visit, and the Rec-reation Lodge. At road's end is the beau-tiful Poplar Tree Lake, a scenic spot with

lakeside picnic tables, a boat launch and dock where jon boats can be rented, a big playground, and a Nature Center. The Nature Center, open seasonally, has animal exhibits, fish aquariums, a bone and insect table, a Native American exhibit, an outdoor aviary, and a butterfly garden behind the center. Small boats with electric trolling motors, canoes, and kayaks are allowed on the lake, and fishing is good both on the lake and along the banks. Largemouth bass, bluegill, and catfish are commonly caught here.

On a nearby side road, reaching out on a peninsula of Poplar Tree Lake, are six rental cabins. These rustic cabins have two bedrooms, outdoor decks, grills, and picnic tables. A pathway from the cabins leads to the lake and a concrete fishing area. Nearby, another side road travels to one of the park's larger shelters, Shelter 5, ideal for group gatherings, with a private setting and ample parking.

Meeman-Shelby Forest State Park offers many interpretative programs, activities, hikes, and trips. The visitor center has a listing of these. Popular activities include pontoon boat rides, ranger-led canoe trips in the cypress swamp, hikes with park naturalists, and pioneer living demonstrations. Managed hunts are also conducted in the park, led by the Tennessee Wildlife Resource Agency. Meeman-Shelby covers a broad area so expect a long drive from one section of the park to another through the extensive forestland. On leaving the park make a stop at the old Shelby Forest General Store, a rustic replica of a 1930s country store in a picturesque setting, known for its sandwiches and hamburgers..

Fort Pillow State Park

West Tennessee - Lauderdale County
Park Address: 3122 Park Road, Henning, TN 38041
Park Size: 1,642 acres   Month Visited: June
Directions: Follow I-40 loop above Memphis, exit Hwy 300
West into Hwy 51 toward Millington. Continue north on Hwy 51
through Millington and Covington, turning west on Hwy 87/371
at Henning. After passing West Tennessee State Penitentiary and
Cold Creek Grocery, turn right on Crutcher Lake Road to park.

Park Description:

Fort Pillow is a historic park, 40 miles from Memphis on the bluffs
overlooking the Mississippi River. The original fort, built by Confederate troops
in 1861, and no longer standing, was a major strategic point during the Civil
War (1861-1865). At the park's office and museum, visitors can learn about the
history of the area, the troops once stationed at Fort Pillow, and about the 1864
battle that took place on the site. The museum has Civil War cannons, photos,
interpretive panels, and artifacts and is interesting to visit. A video about the
1864 battle is available.

At the end of the parking lot is one of the park's trails, leading up to
the 1864 battle point location. Side trails near the museum lead to rifle pits, or
breastworks, historical markers, the former location of the Command Headquarters, and roadways that once latticed the fort area. Further down the road from
the office are other historic sites and more rifle works with markers or kiosks

for explanations. In May the park offers an annual Civil War Living History Day, giving the public a chance to see what life was like for Civil War soldiers, and on the Fourth of July and it provides a patriotic day of outdoor programs.

Within the park are also picnic shelters, a campground, playground, lake with boat ramp, fishing pier, and 20 miles of hiking trails. The children's playground and picnic area on a hillside is especially nice with restrooms and a big pavilion for groups. The campground has 32 sites, six that can accommodate RVs. Fort Pillow also has a group camp that can host up to 200 campers, popular with area scouts, school and church groups. Sullivan's Lake is a scenic spot and good for fishing. The park stocks the lake with bass, bream, and crappie and the 32 acres lake has an easily accessible boat ramp and a large fishing pier. Visitors can bring boats or rent canoes through the park museum office.

History Note:

Early in the Civil War, the Confederacy built Fort Pillow, named for war hero General Gideon J. Pillow, on the Mississippi River as a part of their military defense system. The fort was built high on the Chickasaw bluffs with a battery of cannons facing the river and an extensive system of rifle pits dug to protect the fort and cannons in case of land attack. The Union Army attacked and took

control of the fort for most of the war but in 1864 Colonel Nathan Bedford Forrest led his Confederate troops to take back the fort in what turned out to be a bloody and controversial battle. In the 1970s, Fort Pillow was added

to the National Register of Historic places and designated as a National Historic Landmark.

Reelfoot Lake State Park

West Tennessee - Lake and Obion Counties
Park Address: 2595 Highway 21 East, Tiptonville, TN 38079
Park Size: 404 acres   Month Visited: June
Directions: From I-40 at Jackson, take Hwy 45W north to Union City in the northwest corner of the state. Turn left on Hwy 22 to Reelfoot Lake and then right on Hwy 21 to park visitor center.

Park Description:

Reelfoot Lake is located in the northwest corner of Tennessee. The lake preserve encompasses 25,000 acres, 15,000 of which are water. Bald cypress and cypress knees dominate the margins of the lake but a wide variety of other trees and shrubs are prevalent, with many species of flowers and a diverse array of wildlife. Reelfoot Lake, and designated areas on its shores, are jointly managed by the Tennessee State Park System and the U.S. Fish and Wildlife Services (USFWS). Reelfoot Lake State Park, established in 1956, manages 404 acres scattered around the lake's 22 miles of shoreline in ten segments.

The history of the lake is fascinating. Reelfoot Lake was formed from the New Madrid Earthquakes of 1811-1812. In December 1811, the force of a shock centered in the Reelfoot Lake area, at that time a huge cypress forest, caused the earth's surface to rise and fall, forcibly pushing a rampage of water from the Mississippi River into a newly sunken area of the forest created by the quake. More than 15,000 acres of forest were quickly submerged in water, filling the area and sweeping over 50 species of fish into the basin as well. After the quake, all trees and vegetation underwater soon died except for the cypress and willow trees, which flourished, creating an eerie cypress lake 5-20 feet deep and a natural fish hatchery.

The place to begin a visit of Reelfoot Lake State Park is at the visitor center in the R. C. Donaldson Memorial Museum. At our visit, a new visitor center was under construction and a new park sign being constructed. The current museum and visitor center has maps and brochures, an exhibit area, and a gift shop. Visitors can pick up an auto tour brochure and information about the park's history, legends, and events. From May 1st to September 15th, and during special park events, Reelfoot Lake Scenic Boat Cruises are also available. One hour and three hour cruises are of-

fered with experienced naturalists. Seasonally and with various events, the park also offers bus tours, guided canoe cruises, and interpretive programs and hikes. The center's building contains meeting space for groups, and outside the facility is a Rehab Raptor Center where injured eagles, hawks, and owls are kept and cared for until they can return to the wild.

Behind the center a sidewalk heads to a long, half-mile scenic boardwalk out into Reelfoot Lake. This is an easy walk for all ages leading to overlooks across the expanse of the lake. The trail walks out through bald cypress tree groves and marshy areas full of green duckweed spreading over the water's surface, swamp grasses, water lilies, and other native plants. Water birds may be seen from the park boardwalks and along the banks of the lake—Blue Heron, Great White Egrets, and American Pelican—depending on the season. Reelfoot Lake is located in the Mississippi Flyway for migratory birds, bringing many interesting species of birds through the park. From December to March, the lake is a hot spot for eagle watching. Hundreds of eagles return to their nests at the lake, and visitors can watch eagles flying and soaring over the water and swooping down to catch fish. The park holds its Annual Bald Eagle Festival and Eagle Watch during these months and offers guided Eagle Tours to see the eagle nests in the lake. During the year, eagles may also be spotted in the park as approximately 35 eagles make their home year-round at Reelfoot.

Not far down the road from the visitor center is the park's South Campground and a spillway area that helps regulate the flow of water in the lake. The campground lies directly on the

Reelfoot Lake State Park:

* Visitor Center * Museum * Gift Shop * Rehab Raptor Center * Fishing
* Lake Boardwalk * Guided Canoe & Eagle Tours * Camping/RV Sites
* Cabins * Auto Tour * Picnic Areas * Fishing Piers

lake in a beautiful location and has 86 sites, a check-in station, two bathhouses with showers, a laundry and a dump station. Visitors can also enjoy the playground, pavilion, shady walkways around the park, a fishing pier, and a nice boat launch. A walking trail leads to the seven nearby park cabins, newly constructed and fully furnished, each with lovely outdoor decks.

In this busier south area of the park are privately owned lodges, small lakeside resorts, and a motel, plus a few restaurants, several with a long history at the lake like Boyette's and the Lakeview Restaurant. Heading around the lake on its eastern side leads through the old historic community of Samburg and to the Kirby Pocket, another of the state park segments. At the Kirby Pocket is a giant fish statue—unexpected—a boat launch, an old dock, picnic tables, and views out over the Buck Basin area of the lake.

Fishing is the most popular recreational activity at Reelfoot, off the park piers, from the banks, and in boats out on the lake, although caution is needed navigating the waters among the trees. Crappie fishing is best March to May, largemouth bass from March to October, striped jack or yellow bass July to September, and bream, bluegill and catfish seasonally. The lake is called "a fisherman's paradise" with 54 species of fish thriving in the lake.

Heading around Reelfoot, following the park's auto tour, leads past the USFWS office and visitor center, also offering a variety of activities. The road swings around the backside of Reelfoot, past a Refuge Boundary, and to a side road into the northern Air Park Area. On the Upper Blue Basin, this is the more

primitive area of the park. The Airpark Inn with its own airport runway, scenic balconies looking out over the wetlands and a restaurant, was built here adjacent to the lake in the early 1970s. The Air Park Area included a campground, swimming pool, tennis court, picnic pavilion, picnic grounds, boat launch, and hiking trail. Because of the airstrip, the area once attracted hundreds of visitors. Many called it a nature lover's paradise, but a fire destroyed much of the inn and the building was demolished in 2015. The Reelfoot State Park Airpark Campground, a quiet secluded area, is still open, with 14 sites on two loop roads, restrooms and showers, a dump station, picnic tables and grills. The 1.5 miles Airpark Trail leads through the woods near the campground, and a boat launch can be accessed about a half mile down the road.

Dropping down the west side of Reelfoot leads past the New Markham area near the Waterfowl Refuge and the Black Bayou. A two miles trail called The Black Bayou Trail winds into the old bayou for wildlife and bird observation. Cottonmouth snakes and mosquitoes love these bayou trails, and a watchful eye and bug repellent are good ideas here and in most all sections of this bottomland cypress forest area.

The last park section we visited was on the south side of the lake again, the Keystone Pocket, a scenic spot on a small bay with a boat launch, fishing pier, and a 1.5 miles easy hiking trail along the lakeside. To find this park segment, watch for Keystone Road off the highway. It is only a short distance from the Keystone Pocket back to the visitor center again, full circle around Reelfoot Lake. Visiting this park was a fascinating adventure and a fitting conclusion for our explorations of the Tennessee State Parks.

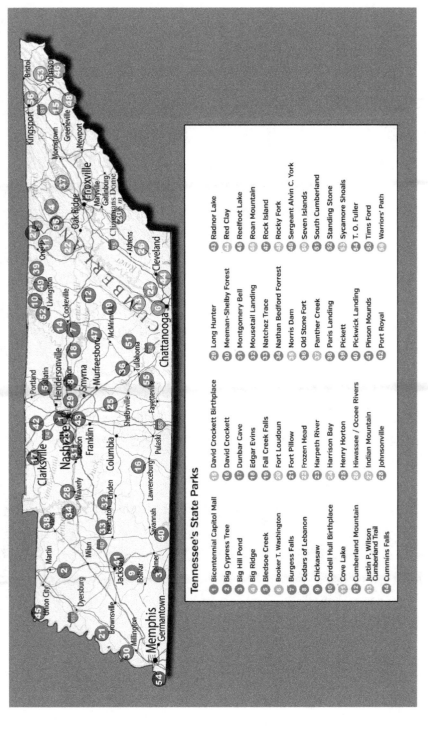

Tennessee's State Parks

1. Bicentennial Capitol Mall
2. Big Cypress Tree
3. Big Hill Pond
4. Big Ridge
5. Bledsoe Creek
6. Booker T. Washington
7. Burgess Falls
8. Cedars of Lebanon
9. Chickasaw
10. Cordell Hull Birthplace
11. Cove Lake
12. Cumberland Mountain
13. Justin P. Wilson Cumberland Trail
14. Cummins Falls

15. David Crockett Birthplace
16. David Crockett
17. Dunbar Cave
18. Edgar Evins
19. Fall Creek Falls
20. Fort Loudoun
21. Fort Pillow
22. Frozen Head
23. Harpeth River
24. Harrison Bay
25. Henry Horton
26. Hiwassee / Ocoee Rivers
27. Indian Mountain
28. Johnsonville

29. Long Hunter
30. Meeman-Shelby Forest
31. Montgomery Bell
32. Mousetail Landing
33. Natchez Trace
34. Nathan Bedford Forrest
35. Norris Dam
36. Old Stone Fort
37. Panther Creek
38. Paris Landing
39. Pickett
40. Pickwick Landing
41. Pinson Mounds
42. Port Royal

43. Radnor Lake
44. Red Clay
45. Reelfoot Lake
46. Roan Mountain
47. Rock Island
48. Rocky Fork
49. Sergeant Alvin C. York
50. Seven Islands
51. South Cumberland
52. Standing Stone
53. Sycamore Shoals
54. T. O. Fuller
55. Tims Ford
56. Warriors' Path

ALPHABETICAL STATE PARK INDEX

Other Books By The Authors

**Other Guide
Books by
the Authors
*The
Afternoon
Hiker***

**Newest
Lin Stepp
Smoky Mtn
Novel
*Lost
Inheritance***

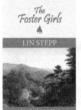
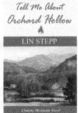

The Foster Girls   *Makin' Miracles*
Tell Me About Orchard Hollow   *Saving Laurel Springs*
For Six Good Reasons   *Welcome Back*
Delia's Place   *Daddy's Girl*
Second Hand Rose   *Lost Inheritance*
Down By The River

Tennessee Fishing & Hunting Guide Magazine

**by J.L. Stepp
Printed Monthly
Or Online at *www.tnfhg.com***

About The Authors

Lin Stepp is a *New York Times* and *USA Today* Best-Selling international author. A native Tennessean, she also works as both a businesswoman and an educator. She is on adjunct faculty at Tusculum College where she has taught research and a variety of psychology and counseling courses for 18 years. Her business background includes over 25 years in marketing, sales, production art, and regional publishing. She has editorial and writing experience in regional magazines and in the academic field. Stepp writes engaging, heart-warming contemporary Southern fiction with a strong sense of place and has eleven published novels, each set in different locations around the Smoky Mountains. Her latest Smokies novels are *Lost Inheritance* (2018), and *Daddy's Girl (2017)*. Previous novels included *Welcome Back* (2016), *Saving Laurel Springs* (2015), *Makin' Miracles* (2015) and *Down by the River* (2014) published by Kensington of New York. Other earlier titles include: *Second Hand Rose* (2013), *Delia's Place* (2012), *For Six Good Reasons* (2011), *Tell Me About Orchard Hollow* (2010), and *The Foster Girls* (2009). In addition, Stepp has co-authored a Smoky Mountains hiking guidebook, also, titled *The Afternoon Hiker*. For more about Stepp's fictional work see: *www.linstepp.com*

J.L. Stepp is the co-author of the best-selling Smoky Mountains hiking guidebook titled *The Afternoon Hiker*. The guidebook features 110 trails descriptions and over 300 color photos. A native East Tennessean, Stepp owns S & S Communications, established in 1990, which publishes a monthly outdoor magazine called *Tennessee Fishing & Hunting Guide*. The magazine covers fishing and hunting topics in Tennessee and is distributed in print form to advertisers at the first of every month. The magazine can also be downloaded from the web by going to *www.tnfhg.com*. J.L., a graduate of The University of Tennessee, also markets UT Vols sports related products such as football and basketball schedules, limited edition prints, and licensed sports collectibles. Stepp's background includes over 45 years in sales, marketing, management, and publications. He enjoys a wide variety of outdoor sports, including golf, fishing, and hiking. Stepp and his wife are currently making plans for a third regional guidebook.

CPSIA information can be obtained
at www.ICGtesting.com
Printed in the USA
LVHW081128290622
722369LV00002B/5